The Importance of
Being Micheál

Micheál MacLiammóir, 1953

THE IMPORTANCE OF BEING MICHEÁL

A Portrait of MacLiammóir

MICHEÁL Ó hAODHA

BRANDON

First published in 1990 by
Brandon Book Publishers Ltd
Cooleen, Dingle, Co Kerry.

British Library Cataloguing in Publication Data
O hAodha, Micheal
The importance of being Micheál: a portrait of Mac Liammóir.
    1. Theatre. Acting. MacLiammóir, Micheál 1899-1978
    I. Title
    792'.028'0924

    ISBN 0-86322-106-8

This book is published with the financial assistance of the Arts Council/
An Chómhairle Ealaíon, Ireland

Photo credits: G.A. Duncan (ii, 116, 119, 121, 124); Gate Theatre (115, 117, 118, 122, 123); Dublin City Archive (115); Camera Press (116); Lensmen (124); *Irish Press* (126); Fergus Bourke (192).

Cover designed by The Graphiconies, Dublin
Typeset by Seton Music Graphics, Bantry, Cork
Printed in England by Clays Ltd, St Ives plc

"What's Hecuba to him, or he to Hecuba
that he should weep for her?"

Hamlet

Contents

List of Illustrations

To all who founded little theatres —
Ba mhór a saothar ar son Hecuba

Acknowledgements

Grateful acknowledgement is due to Richard Pine, editor of the catalogue for the Gate Theatre Golden Jubilee Exhibition, 1978, which provided a ready and reliable reference source. Ulick O'Connor kindly lent copies of his correspondence with Mac-Liammóir; Carmel and Shiela Leahy were more than generous in allowing the use of letters and the reproduction of *The Madonna of the Roads*. MacLiammóir's niece, Mary Rose McMaster, helped greatly with her memories of her uncle and of her father, Anew. Michael Travers was an unfailing helper, giving on loan the correspondence of his aunt, Sally Travers, and early family photographs and illustrations.

Among others who gave help and advice were the late Michael Scott, Dr Patrick Willmore, Gus Smith, Francis Stuart, Eoin Neeson, Padraic O'Farrell, An tOllamh Seán Ó Tuama, Liam Ó Laoghaire, Cyril Cusack, Christopher Fitzsimon, Donncha Ó Dulaing, Vincent Sheridan, Fr Desmond Forrestal, Fr Sean Quigley, Mary Clarke of the Dublin Theatre Archive, Michael Costello of Kerry County Library, Leni McCullagh of the RTE Visuals Library, Peter Malone and Steve MacDonogh of Brandon Book Publishers.

Finally, a word of thanks to a helper who prefers to remain anonymous. To my knowledge he is the only person to have read the original manuscripts of MacLiammóir's personal diaries, written in Irish and now held in the Gate Theatre Archive in North Western University, Illinois. This reader informed me that the diaries seemed hurriedly written and consisted of rough notes for what was later published in *Ceo Meala Lá Seaca*, *Aisdeoirí faoi Dhá Solas*, *Put Money in Thy Purse* and *Each Actor on His Ass*. To the publishers of these books and other works listed in the bibliography, I wish to express my thanks; Thames and Hudson very kindly permitted the reproduction of extracts from *Enter a Goldfish* and Michael Williams, executor of the MacLiammóir/Edwards estate, extracts from *All for Hecuba* and the painting and stage designs on pages 113 and 114.

Micheál Ó hAodha
August 1990

· PROLOGUE ·

A Famous First Night

THE IMPORTANCE OF BEING OSCAR, Micheál MacLiammóir's triumphant one-man show, was first performed to an audience of about two hundred at the Gaelic Hall of the Curragh Military Camp in County Kildare. The visit had been arranged with the army authorities by an old friend of MacLiammóir's, Kildare solicitor Jack Dunne. The squat concrete building was an unlikely venue for such an important preview, but here MacLiammóir played and for a full two-and-a-half hours he "harangued the troops on the subject of Oscar Wilde". He received a warm reception from the invited audience, a response which was reassuring to an actor embarking, with some trepidation, on his first attempt at a one-man show. Four days later, on 19 September 1960, MacLiammóir gave his first public performance of *The Importance of Being Oscar* at the Gaiety Theatre in Dublin.

The curtain rose on a table, a sofa and a pedestal with an urn of great waxen moonlit lilies, placed on an octagonal carpet of violet and gold. On the sofa reclined MacLiammóir in evening dress with a green carnation in his buttonhole. Out of the half-light came a voice of molten gold reciting "Helas":

To drift with every passion until my soul
Is a stringed lute on which all winds can play.
Is it for this that I have given away
Mine ancient wisdom and austere control?
Methinks my life is a twice-written scroll
Scrawled over on some boyish holiday
With idle songs for pipe and virelay
Which do but mar the secret of the whole.

MacLiammóir's own account of many of his triumphs may be a palimpsest, "a twice-written scroll", but this first-night *Importance of Being Oscar* was his apotheosis. Hilton Edwards' account of the performance of his partner was, befitting a director, both sober and informative.

MacLiammóir's range as an actor equals the variety of his talents, but he possesses a gift for which the formality of the legitimate theatre seems to offer little scope. As much as an actor, he is an entertainer; a raconteur. His clouded-velvet voice, his exceptional capacity for appreciation, his gaiety and ready wit, all make him a spell-binder. Whatever his skill as an interpreter of the creations of others, he seems to attain fulfilment only when he is juggling with ideas and words of his own selection. The *Seanchaí*, the story-teller, is a fast vanishing figure in the tradition of Gaelic and Irish culture. Oscar Wilde, though possibly unaware of it, owed much of his influence both as an artist and a social lion to the craft of the *Seanchaí*.

MacLiammóir also shares something of the secret of this craft. Possessing a talent so little dependent on the complex machinery of theatrical production, it is not surprising that he was urged to the consideration of a solo performance; to seek a form that would permit him a freedom larger than that of interpretation alone. . . .

As the project took shape I became convinced that in performance the actor's involvement must be limited; at no moment should the actor *play*, that is to say impersonate Oscar Wilde. He could identify himself with Wilde's theories and emotions; he could temporarily become the characters of Wilde's creation, but he must never attempt to be Wilde but must remain always himself. Stepping, as it were, in and out of the picture as occasion demanded he yet must always maintain an attitude aloof and ultimately objective; that is the Teller of the Story, the *Seanchaí*.[1]

This reference to MacLiammóir as a *seanchaí* was greatly to his liking; it made him part of a centuries-old Irish tradition. The *seanchaí*, a spellbinder with words, displayed a keen sense of the dramatic, even if it was by a fireside rather than on a stage that he practised his craft. He too favoured a solo performance, a one-man show, preferring to fashion the story himself rather than share the dialogue with others.

Before going on stage MacLiammóir had felt an impending sense of doom and in the first moments after the curtain rose he was obsessed by the fear that if he were once to step off the magic carpet of violet and gold he would be hurled headlong into space. But he had come through those moments of dread and, as he moved effortlessly from high comedy to tragic intensity, Dublin saw MacLiammóir at his magnificent best. For the actor — the *seanchaí* — the first night of *The Importance of Being Oscar* was a "reingreencarnation"; his performance was acclaimed as a triumph.

The life of this great and greatly admired man of the Irish theatre attained an unusual sense of completeness with his creation of *The Importance of Being Oscar*. As well as crafting a magnificent representation of the life and work of Oscar Wilde, he had succeeded in using the figure of Wilde as the final element in the forging of his own identity. From an early age he had seemed to pay heed to Wilde's dictum that "The first duty in life is to assume a pose". In his long career as an actor he went far beyond striking a pose. The greatest of all the distinguished parts he played was not that of Hamlet, of Robert Emmet, of Iago or even of Oscar Wilde in ectoplasm, but the creation of the character known as Micheál MacLiammóir.

· I ·

Exit a Goldfish

I believe that while we are alive we lie to protect ourselves from the truth itself. The lies we tell are part of the life we live and therefore part of the truth.

Michael Holroyd *Bernard Shaw: The Search for Love*

I T WAS GENERALLY accepted during his lifetime that Micheál MacLiammóir was Irish and had been born in Ireland — in Blackrock, a suburb of Cork City, on 25 October 1899. His original surname of Willmore he had changed on reaching adulthood to an Irish version. But despite what we are told in his autobiographies and in reference books, there is no mention of any Willmore in the Cork Register of Births, Deaths and Marriages for the closing years of the last century. Moreover, no Willmore is mentioned in the standard reference books, Edward MacLysaght's *Irish Families* and Woulfe's *Irish Names and Surnames*. In MacLysaght's *Supplement to Irish Families* he comments that the name in its Gaelic form of MacLiammóir is well known solely because of the international reputation of the actor. He quotes an authority, Bardsley, who equated Willmore with the English name Wilmer. MacLysaght adds, "Though I have not met any near-Gaelic Anglicized form of the name I cannot state for certain that it is not Irish in origin; it occurs in County Tyrone in 1596, when Anne Willmore received a *pardon*." [1]

In his first autobiographical work, *All for Hecuba*, MacLiammóir stated that all his father's people were of Munster origin.

Many of my forebears had come from Clare to Limerick and then to Cork to grind corn before they took themselves to London to sell flour, and I took an egoist's pleasure in hoping that some of the qualities of these gaunt solitudes had entered into my blood, and had had as much to do with my composition as the drowsy, flower-grown walls of Cork, where the inconsequential years had passed, or the plane-shadowed asphalt and the rattling milk-carts of the London suburb where I had begun to grow up. [2]

Elsewhere he mentioned that his paternal grandfather had been a native Irish speaker from near Ennistymon in County Clare who had "never had much regard for the language". However, Edward MacLysaght was himself from Clare and would have known of any Willmore from that county or the neighbouring county of Limerick.

An expert in Cork family history, the late Eoin "Pope" O'Mahony, had no knowledge of any Cork residents named Willmore but felt that, while the Willmore family did not come originally from Cork, it was possible that they might have lived in Cork for a short period, as many who worked in Cork's milling industry and, indeed, in the army commissariat had come from England in the last century and up to the time of the First World War.

Those who knew Micheál MacLiammóir and those who wrote about him either accepted what he said about his origins at face value or exhibited varying degrees of confusion. Two of his long-time friends in Cork were Sean and Geraldine Neeson. Sean was the first Director of the Cork Broadcasting Station where Geraldine was piano accompanist. Geraldine first met Micheál in 1927 but although she had herself been born in Cork City she had no knowledge of his supposed birth and early childhood in the Blackrock suburb. Amongst those who wrote about him Seamus Kelly, of *The Irish Times*, stated that Micheál was born in West Cork. Stephen Gwynn in *Irish Literature and Drama* gave an even less likely place of origin — the Aran Islands. No one questioned the apparent fact that Micheál MacLiammóir was Irish, but one person who hinted broadly that his account of his birthplace might not be entirely true was MacLiammóir's brother-in-law, Anew McMaster. "Show me the house in Cork," he would say in a bantering way, "where Micheál was born, and I'll give you a hundred pounds."

The truth of the matter is that he was indeed born on 25 October 1899, but not in Cork, nor even in Ireland. He was born instead at 150 Purves Road, Willesden, London, to Mary Elizabeth Willmore, formerly Lee, and her husband Alfred Willmore, whose occupation was given on the birth certificate as a Forage Dealer's Buyer. He was named Alfred Lee Willmore.

There is no evidence that Alfred Willmore Senior had any Irish background, though there are enigmatic and contradictory traces of a Spanish family connection. He was born on 23 May 1863 at 7 Upper Gloucester Road, Marylebone, London, and was given two quintessentially English names: Alfred George. On his birth certificate his mother is named as Eliza Willmore and no father's name is given, suggesting that she may not have been married at the time. However, when Alfred George Willmore married Mary Elizabeth Lee at the parish church in Camberwell on 12 January 1888, his father's name and occupation were given as Alfred Willmore, corn merchant. Amongst the family photographs in Micheál MacLiammóir's possession was one which he had captioned: Maria Carmen Morena y Dacosta; Hilton Edwards understood this to have been Micheál's father's mother. On the evidence of the birth certificate he must have been mistaken, but MacLiammóir certainly referred to a Spanish grand-aunt on his father's side. She was Luisa Conception Fuentes, and both Alfred Senior and Alfred Junior visited her, according to MacLiammóir's account, in Seville in 1914.

In his autobiographical books MacLiammóir gave only a very sketchy picture of his family and the circumstances in which he grew up. The remarks about his early years supposedly spent in Cork are just that — remarks rather than pictures; the reader is never drawn into the world of his childhood. It is also impossible to gain from the books any clear picture of his parents. His mother, Mary Elizabeth Lawler Lee, is an indistinct figure; he presented her as being Irish but never referred specifically to her antecedents, though he mentioned distant cousins on her side of the family called Ryan and O'Keefe. He wrote of her affectionately but vaguely as if she had been a typical Mother Machree, later calling her by the family pet name of Sophie.

Her background is somewhat obscure. On her marriage certificate her father's name was given as Frederick Lee and his occupation as corn merchant, while on her birth certificate he was named as Robert Samuel Lee and described as a working jeweller living in Islington. Her mother was named Rebecca, formerly Essex. The records, rather than confirming an Irish connection, seem to indicate an English Jewish background.

MacLiammóir's neice, Mary Rose McMaster, has with admirable clarity placed in context the untruths and ambiguities of his accounts of his origins and family background:

I think his writing is sometimes "over-blown" and in his autobiographies he was prone to distorting facts and exaggeration! Some of this had to do with his great need to belong in every way to Ireland which he passionately loved as you know, but like many patriots before him, he had "alien" blood in his veins.[3]

*　　*　　*

Memories of childhood recollected in old age by MacLiammóir resembled scenes from a toy theatre, not penny plain but twopence coloured. Very little is known for certain about those early years apart from what he wrote in *Enter a Goldfish*. Even those "Memoirs of an Actor, Young and Old", as he called them, show an innate tendency to dramatize, to mystify, even to hide. The other members of his family had their entrances and their exits, they often had good lines to deliver, but they remained supporting players in a domestic drama where little Alfred was destined to top the bill.

One small and enigmatic sub-plot in the drama of Alfred's childhood is given a great deal of emphasis in Micheál Mac-Liammóir's *Enter a Goldfish*. The book begins with the music and words of a song:

I'se a going to bite you, I'se a going to bite you.

I'se a going to bite you, all down here.

And the powerful baritone whisper grew louder and softer, the smooth palm stroking the little boy's body under the sheet grew deeper and lighter, and slowly it faded and the child was asleep again . . .[4]

This passage in the opening chapter entitled "A dream of childhood" represented his earliest memory, a recurring nightmare about "Daddy with the Hard Hat". The overtones of psycho-sexual fantasy are clear, but what is not clear is how much this account owed to MacLiammóir's or young Alfred's overheated imagination, or how much derived from ambiguities of his own inner nature. That it constituted a repeated fantasy of some considerable importance is indicated by the fact that not only does he open the book with this song but he also closes the book with it.

MacLiammóir's picture of his father is otherwise of an easygoing, pipe-smoking man whose concerns were those of a businessman whose business was going through rough times for most of Alfred's childhood. For the most part life at 150 Purves Road, Willesden, was frugally comfortable for a little boy with a doting mother and four sisters all older than himself. Dorothy, the eldest sister, was a beauty, an aloof star in the play for children which his autobiographical account resembles. Next came Christine (Tina), a terror in her mother's eyes and up to no good in Alfred Junior's. The third sister, tiny Marjorie (Maimie and later Mana) was fair as a cowslip, not good looking and showing signs of anorexia. The poor girl, on whom Alfred in his role as Little Boy Blue depended greatly, is cast in the writing as an *iarlais*, a changeling child, in contrast to the youngest sister, Peg, a high-principled young lady who seemed destined for Wagnerian roles. Little Alfred was six years younger than Peg, so nursery plays like *The Sleeping Beauty* were not always cast to his satisfaction. In one of these he received his first notice as an actor — from the critic Christine: "That child's lisp," she declared, "is not only not improving, 'tis getting worse."[5]

Lisp or no lisp, Alfred was marched off to free primary, or council school at Willesden. Here, according to his own account, he was called "Irish", "Paddywack" and "Curly"; but this we may safely regard as one of his minor distortions. In fact, it was probably amongst the four hundred youngsters in the school that he gained his first introduction to Ireland and the Irish. He won a prize for a composition but was hopeless at sums, and overall he was most unhappy. Hilton Edwards suggested that he was an obvious butt for the toughs:

"Get out on the field and kick the ball," yelled the master in a markedly Cockney accent. Young Micheál does so — through his own goal — and got the bird for the first and only time.[6]

Willesden primary school proved unbearable and after little more than a year there Alfred was withdrawn by his parents. He studied at home with the help of Christine's and Marjorie's tuition and was thus saved from the rigours of a formal education. Those early years in Willesden were, according to Hilton Edwards, "a period of near poverty", during which his father was experiencing severe financial difficulties, and his few months at a council school left "a small but lasting scar".[7]

At home Alfred took to acting before the long mirror in his parents' bedroom with only his reflection in the glass for an audience. His repertoire included pieces from Lamb's *Tales from Shakespeare* and improvisations of "lurid and impassioned speeches, bodily contortions and frenzied gesticulations as he mouthed scene after scene of treachery, of thwarted love, of deaths from poisoned cups or daggers or lightning bolts".[8] Some of these performances were the result of Christine's tuition.

His father knew a few people on the theatrical fringe and brought along an old acquaintance one day to eavesdrop on the solo star. Impressed by the performance, the friend suggested an audition with "the Chief" — Sir Herbert Beerbohm Tree, actor-manager and owner of His Majesty's Theatre.

"So, Boy Blue, you are going to perform for me. What can you do? Can you stand on your head?"

"I can't, Sir Herbert."

"Oh, what a pity! Can you juggle?"

"I don't think so."

"No? Perhaps you can dance a hornpipe?"

"No, I can't, Sir Herbert."

"It's a pity, but there are other qualifications. Now tell me, if you can't stand on your head, and you can't juggle or dance a hornpipe . . . what in Heaven's name can you do?"

"Oh, I can act."

"But how interesting! Because only a few people can. Well, will you act for me?"

"I will, of course."

"I shall disappear in the stalls with Mr Weldon, Mr King and Mr Dana and you will go with Mr Pickens here to the stage." [9]

In the Irish version of this incident in *Ceo Meala Lá Seaca*, Tree adds: "You're Irish aren't you; very good. I like the Irish. Out and out devils. But they speak good English." [10]

Alfred's audition choice was the wooing scene from *The Taming of the Shrew*, in which he played Petruchio and Katherine. As in fairy tales and the reminiscences of child actors, Alfred heard the magic words from Tree: "You will be an actor". Turning to Alfred's father he added: "I should like your boy to play in my beautiful theatre. Remind me, Mr Dana." [11]

While he waited for a call from Sir Herbert, his mother sent his photograph to Miss Lila Field who was casting a children's play, *The Goldfish*. This was in reply to an advertisement in the *Daily Telegraph* offering auditions for "pretty, intelligent children, from eight to eighteen". Alfred secured the leading part of King Goldfish at a salary of two pounds a week. A boy named Noel Coward had a minor role; he seemed a little too sure of himself, Alfred thought.

The *Daily Express* of 25 January 1911 noted that "a little boy — Master Alfred Willmore — is a finished little actor, and has great ambitions. But his pet name is 'Bubbles' for he has the little angel face and the golden curls of the child in Millais' famous picture."

The *Morning Post* was more critical, finding the talk very trying: "not the speech of childhood. Master Alfred Willmore played with the utmost sang-froid". The critic was not in the least put out by "the annoying behaviour of his socks and curls. His socks kept coming down and when he bent to pull them up, his curls of which he had a glorious crop, fell forward over his eyes and no sooner was he occupied with clearing his eyes than one or other of the socks again took advantage of the fact." However, in the second act he exchanged the socks for tights and "could now give his part undivided attention".

The *Daily News* found it "delightful to listen to the clear enunciation of little Alfred Willmore who in addition delivered his song 'A Prisoner I' with fine assumption and manly bravado".

Noel Coward cannot have been pleased to read that "among the other tiny artists who deserve a congratulatory pat on the back are Miss Noel Coward, Miss Nellie Terriss and Miss Peggy Bryant". At rehearsals Noel had informed Alfred that there was "nothing as good as the theatre — that is, if you're made for it". But he did not like the idea of singing other people's songs to other people's music, so he dedicated to Bubbles a verse of his own which he was about to set to music.

I see you are bent on the stage
All efforts to restrain you I fear would be in vain
You will fly like a bird from the cage
And we may never see you again.

By the end of the run of *The Goldfish*, Alfred Willmore was indeed enchanted by the magic of the crystal bowl called theatre.

That summer the society magazine, *The Lady*, reported that Master Willmore appeared (by permission of Miss Lila Field) in a charming little play, *Fly Away Land*, staged at the Queen's Gate Hall in aid of the Cripple Boys' Home.

When the call came from Beerbohm Tree's secretary offering a part in *Macbeth*, Alfred was glad to be working with real actors at last. Opening in late September 1911, he doubled the parts of MacDuff's son and the Second Apparition: a Bloody Child. He was mentioned favourably in the reviews but there was a real "scoop" when the *Evening News* published a drawing, initialled A.W., of "Master Willmore as he sees himself with Lady MacDuff". The notice went on to refer to a fine collection of Macbeth sketches by this eleven-year-old boy. Alfred was now earning two pounds and ten shillings a week — more than his sisters who had "nice" jobs as shop assistants. In later life MacLiammóir often reminded interviewers and critics that he had never been an amateur.

His next appearance was at the Duke of York's Theatre where he played Michael in the Christmas 1911 production *Peter Pan*, in which the name part was played by Pauline Chase. The director, Dot Boucicault, was the son of the prodigious actor/ playwright Dion Boucicault whose Irish melodramas, *The Shaughraun*, *The Colleen Bawn* and *Arrah na Pogue* were box-office hits on both sides of the Atlantic. The production, and Alfred's performance in it were pronounced a success and gave rise in his immediate family to the adopting of "Mickie" as his nickname. In 1912 and 1913 the boy actor toured the provinces with the show, which also played in Dublin. He recalled that:

I used to spend a lot of my time at the Abbey Theatre, watching the Irish plays. I think they are fine and I like reading W.B. Yeats's plays.[12]

In none of the various newspaper articles in which he was mentioned at this time of his fame as a child actor was there any mention of him having been born in Cork or of any Irish family connection.

In 1912 he was presented to Sarah Bernhardt after he had appeared in a charity matinée in aid of the survivors of the *Titanic* disaster, and later in the same year his greatest opportunity as a boy actor came with an invitation from Sir Herbert Beerbohm Tree to play the name part in *Oliver Twist* at His Majesty's Theatre. He took full advantage of the opportunity and received the kind of notices that had greeted the child prodigy Master Betty a century earlier when he had upstaged players like Mrs Siddons and John Kemble. Under the heading "Boy Plays Title Part", the *Standard* reported:

Usually played by an actress, the character gained in sincerity and conviction by the experiment. Master Alfred Willmore, the new Oliver, is a curly haired twelve-year-old boy who acted "Michael" in the last revival of *Peter Pan*. The little fellow's Oliver had an appeal which immediately won the audience and his performance was an instantaneous success.[13]

The *Sketch* published a photograph headed "The Youngest Oliver Twist Ever Seen On the Stage":

Master Alfred Willmore, who is playing the name part at His Majesty's, is only eleven, and is said to be the youngest player who has ever appeared in the part. He plays it in a way that wins all hearts.[14]

MacLiammóir's own backstage account was somewhat different:

Rehearsals were strenuous for the boy actor, for it was revealed to him that he didn't know nearly as much about the craft, let alone the art, of acting as he had imagined. This of course was extremely good for him, though the discovery caused a little wounded pride and a certain lack of self-confidence which, like the right amount of salt in a good dish, is necessary to the actor even when he is a child, but fatal if the quantity be too great. Yet everybody was kind to him, and the Chief was the kindest of them all, the most severe of his criticisms being, "You see, Boy Blue, it is perfectly clear to me that you can do it supremely well if you really want to *and* if you will act naturally as a natural if unfortunate boy, not pose in strange and beautiful attitudes as if you were appearing in the Russian — ah! I remember! You told me the other day that you had been watching that damned Russian Ballet! Ah! The great, the unbelievable Nijinsky! But acting is not dancing, Boy Blue, though dancing at moments may include the art of acting; a reversal of this leads to mannerism . . . posing . . . artificiality. . . . Be natural, Boy Blue, be yourself and believe in what you are saying and what Dickens, adapted by Mr Comyns Carr, has given you to say. Your voice is good, your English passable, though you still say "hosse" for house and "aboat" for about . . . still you are doing finely; continue if you must to watch the great Nijinsky . . . and the great Pavlova too — but do not let their art obscure your own.[15]

Beerbohm Tree's criticism of "the pose" was repeated by other reviewers in the next half-century, one of the last to voice the complaint being the distinguished American novelist and critic, Mary McCarthy. It would seem that MacLiammóir did not pay the least notice.

All this publicity and adulation were bound to attract the attention of certain older actors. Orson Welles alleged that

In those days there were all kinds of high-society elderly gentlemen who could be waiting for him with bouquets of flowers when he came out. He'd been *enormously* spoiled because he was the toast of the town, and apparently in the West End it was perfectly alright for a child actor to be a sexual object and carry on like a leading lady.[16]

But Welles was undoubtedly recalling third- or fourth-hand gossip, and although Alfred did attract the attentions of such admirers, he was usually chaperoned by his sister Marjorie.

At the time there were also references to certain "fans" who invited him to go with them to the Russian Ballet. There he was deeply impressed, though it was not Nijinsky whom he tried to imitate, as Tree had suggested, for nobody could resemble Nijinsky:

a being far withdrawn from human life: he was a faun, a rose, a floating star, a tragic puppet, a dark and gilded personification of lust, an aerial abstraction of purity and grace that soared like a dream through the eyes and left the spectator breathless in some region of the spirit he had never known before.[17]

It was Pavlova's partner, Novikoff, who stirred a half-conscious desire in Alfred:

Novikoff, with his muscular build, his splendid virility, his joyful bounding grace. He it was who filled the youthful aspirant for the first time in his life with a pride that he was of the same sex as this Russian dancer . . .[18]

Alfred's career as a boy actor was drawing towards an end when he appeared as Benjamin in *Joseph and His Brethren* by Louis N. Parker, produced by Sir Beerbohm Tree at His Majesty's Theatre in September 1913. But it had been a remarkable career by any standards. Within three years he had established himself in the West End as the outstanding boy actor of his generation. A self-made prodigy, he had never attended a school of acting, or a school of any kind apart from his short unhappy stay at the school at Willesden.

Both Alfred and his sister Marjorie formed a close friend-ship at this time with another young actor, a lovable giant named Anew McMaster. Alfred was enchanted by McMaster, whom he described on a first meeting as "a tall golden-haired absurdly good-looking young man in a pale grey suit". In his own account MacLiammóir included a reference to his Irishness in McMaster's conversation:

"Well, duckie, I've seen you . . . at three different matinées and I don't mind telling you I thought you absolutely splendid. And somebody told me you were Irish. I'm so glad because I am too but from the *North* I'm sorry to say, such dreary pogs they are up there, and I was brought up a Presbyterian, can you believe it?[19]

From his first entrance into the Willmore circle, the older Anew was only too ready to upstage Alfred. Though still in his early twenties his stage experience ranged from musical comedy to Shakespeare, and he never seemed to lack engagements. He was the type of actor who did not care where he acted as long as he was on stage, though preferably in a leading part. As a result he never stayed very long in any one place, though he became an important player in the Willmores' lives.

With the end of a provincial tour of *Peter Pan* in April 1914, Alfred's enchanted youth had ended except for a few child parts in early British films such as *Enoch Arden* and *The Little Minister*. He was now nearly fifteen, his voice had broken and he had outgrown the parts in which he excelled. He was faced with the difficult transition from boy actor to juvenile lead if he were to continue his career on stage. He had shown an early talent for drawing and he seemed more likely at this stage to seek to improve his skills as an artist.

In June 1914 his father decided to take him on a visit to his Spanish grand-aunt, Luisa Conception Fuentes, in Seville. He wanted him, he said, to broaden his horizons by learning Spanish and getting to know more of Europe. After a fortnight his father returned home, leaving Alfred to the tender care of Tia Luisa and his older cousins, Juan and Manuel. They treated him with affection, particularly Juan who made Alfred more than aware of his latent homosexuality during the summer of 1914. Although now nearly fifteen, he had never shown any interest in the beautiful young girls whom he met during his stage career. Until the Spanish interlude, he seems to have been well chaperoned by Marjorie who kept the more passionate of the stage-door "fans", as he called them, at bay in London. Here in Seville the *gitanos*, the tambourines, the castanets, the picadors, *banderillas*, the matadors, the blood and sand made sexual initiation part of the fiesta.

In August, Britain and France declared war on Germany and Alfred was summoned home.

He would never be quite the same person again, but it was not a transformation of human love that he felt, for not one of the members of the family in the Calle San Fernando could ever take the place in his heart that his mother and father and his four sisters held. The intimacy between himself and Juan left nothing behind but a consciousness of his nature that he both resented and accepted as being inevitably within himself. Juan had revealed to him that he was growing up and that he must accept himself as he was, but this was merely a development, not a revolution.[20]

There are no references to sexual exploits in Spain in *Ceo Meala Lá Seaca*. The Irish text is more concerned with the abandon of Spanish dancers and with his admiration for the painting of Murillo and Zurburan. Regarding painting as a higher form of art than acting, he decided on his return from Spain to study art seriously. In *Ceo Meala Lá Seaca* MacLiammóir mentioned the Slade, while no school is named in the memoir in English. In fact, it was at the Willesden Polytechnic, close to his birthplace, that he began his studies.

The article in the *Star* in which young Alfred spoke about Yeats and the Abbey, also mentioned his drawing:

To have attained some measure of success both as an actor and artist, and that at the early age of 15, is an achievement beyond the powers of the average youthful prodigy. Such is the record so far of Alfred Willmore, now a promising student at the Willesden Polytechnic School of Art . . . and only three weeks ago a clever drawing from his pen appeared in *Punch*, that exclusive Academy of black and white artists. And he is still in knickerbockers, a merry boy, with tousled hair and inky fingers.[21]

Reproduced in the article were a pencil drawing of Alfred by a fellow student named Robert Clarke and Alfred's own drawing from the 2 June 1915 issue of *Punch*, "The Damsel I Left Behind Me", which was described as "a Recruiting Poster in the Style of the New Decorative School". It was an extremely competent black and white sketch in the Beardsley manner, but it is doubtful if its impact as a recruiting poster rallied great numbers to enlist in the army. It was Alfred's first and last contribution to the war effort.

The head of the art school, Mr R.T. Mumford, was quoted in the article:

"I was more than a little staggered when he showed me the drawing in *Punch*. None of us had any idea he was contemplating sending his work out. It was a little ambitious to choose that high level for his venture, and to have succeeded is something of which the school is justly proud." [22]

After a short resumé of his acting career the article continued: He has always shown a predilection for art and this gift his parents fostered, ultimately sending him to Willesden School for a proper training.

There is nothing of the youthful prodigy about young Willmore. He is just a healthy boy, full of life, blessed with a fertile imagination and a lot of good looks. His portfolio of drawings is full of impressions of Nijinsky, rough drafts of illustrations for Irish folk and fairy stories, and stray pencilled thoughts suggested by his wide reading. A clever boy, clever far above the average, and all the better for realising how much he has yet to learn.[23]

While studying art, Alfred was to draw learning from an inspirational source:

In the studio where the first year students drew from plaster casts of classical sculptures he saw on his second day a tall girl with dark brown hair, a longish face, and up-slanting, luminous, green-blue eyes that watched him for a moment or two over the corner of the drawing board she held in front of her and then looked away to concentrate on her work. Presently she looked at him again and, he said:

"I've seen you before somewhere, haven't I?"

He really thought he had.

"I was thinking that about you," she answered him.[24]

That evening they met again and ate the still-life pears — "one large, overripe pear apiece" — and, echoing Oscar Wilde, felt "exquisitely guilty". A melodramatic thunderstorm broke:

But although the rain was pouring down into the gutters with the tumultuous music of invisible legions tumbling from the skies, yet all the world seemed for a moment caught up into a mysterious stillness, and there they were, the two of them, journeying slowly through wooded valleys among great mountains under a golden light of the sun.

"It was the Golden Age," he heard her say, and then all was dark again, and they were back at the open window in a darkened room and the rain was pouring down over the London streets.[25]

This girl with whom he shared a dream, and who believed that they had first met in an earlier aeon, was Máire O'Keefe. With an Irish father and English mother, long separated, she had never seen Ireland but, for Alfred, she lived in a time-warp and had been there before:

It was a strange friendship, the only real friendship . . . with a woman who was not his sister. Strange perhaps, because it was so passionless. There was no hint on either side of any romantic excitement, of any sexual curiosity. Yet this background of some remote and beautiful past clung often about them as they sat together at work before their easels at the school, or walked together through the streets or over Hampstead Heath . . .[26]

Máire lived with her mother who was always "craving for things". She now craved a nephew and for a time Alfred filled the part to perfection, so she became Aunt Craven and, later, simply "Craven". Amongst his own family Dorothy, his eldest sister, had married a Welshman named Old and had left home, while Peg, the youngest, spent her time either out working or helping her mother with the housework. Alfred was more interested in the bizarre adventures of his wildest sister, Christine, who had insinuated herself into a Hampstead circle or coven which existed under the aegis of "The Beast", Aleister Crowley. Their father, whose business as a corn merchant or forage agent had been hit by mechanisation, spent a good deal of his time cursing the internal combustion engine.

According to MacLiammóir's own account his father also devoted much time to dreaming of Irish-speaking grandparents who lived somewhere in County Clare. However, this suggestion of Irish antecedents on his side is almost certainly an invention of MacLiammóir's, as were the accounts of his Cork birth and upbringing. Micheál's half-brother, Patrick Willmore, a child of Alfred Senior's second marriage, never heard his father speak about Ireland or about any Irish family connection.

Young Alfred had decided at the age of seventeen that he would become Irish. This would lead to a progressive separation from his true background in England and the creation of an alleged Irish family background. He would not attend his mother's funeral in London in 1918 and he never referred to his father's second marriage; nor did he reveal that he had a half-brother, Patrick (who became a distinguished scientist and head of the Global Seismology Unit at the British Geological Survey in Edinburgh), though he would in 1934 visit London to see his father, who was then in his final illness. Ireland and an Irish identity had become his obsession, an obsession which conflicted with the reality of his evidently English background.

Of his two closest friends one — Anew McMaster — was Irish and the other — Máire O'Keefe — was half-Irish. Identifying with the dashing, handsome young actor who was some nine years his senior and who conveyed such enthusiasm and passion for theatre, Alfred had come to identify Ireland and Irishness with all the positive elements of imagination and creativity which he yearned to explore. He admired Anew enormously and, like many a young person, wanted passionately to be like the object of his admiration. Then Máire O'Keefe spun the web of her imaginative Irish dreamworld around him and he began to dream himself — to dream of Ireland, of the world of the imagination, and of being Irish. He set about the business of his own re-creation, not in any light and self-indulgent manner, but by sitting down with determination and great practical application to the formidable task of learning to speak the Irish language like a native.

The Wearing of the Green

The Greeks looked within their borders, and we like them have a history fuller than any other history of imaginative events; and legends which surpass, as I think, all legends but theirs in wild beauty, and in our land, as in theirs, there is no river or mountain that is not associated in the memory with some event or legend.

W.B. Yeats *Ireland and the Arts*

ALFRED WILLMORE WAS stimulated in his mid-teens to cultivate an Irish identity by the personal influences of Anew McMaster and Máire O'Keefe. The intellectual influence in his Gaelicization came from Yeats. In *Ceo Meala Lá Seaca*, he wrote:

> I went to the Slade School to study painting and about this time I read an essay by a man named Yeats. "Ireland and the Arts" was the title of the essay, and I believe it changed my whole life.[1]

The impulse to learn Irish had come from his reading of this messianic credo in which, as early as 1901, Yeats had set forth his cultural manifesto, combining in a heady mix the unseen world of myth and legend with William Morris's advocacy of the utility of the arts. That Yeats himself neither spoke nor wrote Irish was of no importance to Alfred: the article stimulated a yearning in him and he seized on the language as his first avenue to an Irish identity. Against the background of the secure but somewhat drab and dreary England in which he was born and had grown up, Yeats's words rang like an inspirational clarion call:

> We who care deeply about the arts find ourselves the priesthood of an almost forgotten faith, and we must, I think, if we are to win the people again, take upon ourselves the method and fervour of the priesthood. We must be half humble and half proud. . . . We must baptize as well as preach. . . . The makers of religions have re-named wells and images and given new meaning to the ceremonies of spring and midsummer and harvest. In very early days the arts were almost inseparable from religion, going side by side with it into all life. . . . But here in Ireland, when the arts have grown humble they will find two passions ready to their hands, love of the unseen life and love of country. . . . If he is a painter or a sculptor he will find churches awaiting his art everywhere, and if he follows the masters of his craft, our other passion will come into his art also, for he will show his Holy Family winding among hills like those of Ireland, and his Bearer of the Cross among faces copied from the faces of his own town . . .

Art and scholarship like these I have described would give Ireland more than they received from her, for they would make love of the unseen more unshakeable, more ready to plunge into the abyss, and they would make love of country more fruitful in the mind, more a part of daily life. One would know an Irishman into whose life they had come — and in a few generations they would come into the life of all, rich and poor — by something that set him apart among men. He would understand that more was expected of him than of others, because he had greater possessions. The Irish race would have become a chosen race, one of the pillars that uphold the world.[2]

Inspired by Yeats, the young actor and artist was intent on creating for himself a clearly Gaelic identity which would transcend the mundane realities of Willesden. He pursued his studies enthusiastically at classes run by the Gaelic League in the inappropriately named Ireton House at Ludgate Circus, where his teachers were Seán Ó Cochláin, a kilted enthusiast from West Cork, and Eibhlín Ní hÉigeartaigh from the same area. His first textbook was Miss Norma Borthwick's *Ceachta Beaga Gaeilge* which had charming black and white illustrations by Jack B. Yeats. With the help of Father Dineen's dictionary he was soon reading the vade-mecum of all learners of the Munster dialect, *Séadna*. His mother bought him a copy which he dutifully inscribed in his own hand, *Do Mhiceál ón a Mháthair* — to Micheal from his mother.

He was now reading AE (George Russell), a prophet without a church who was in the process of recreating a Celtic pantheon. Under the influence of Madame Blavatsky, AE had mastered theosophy and introduced his fellow poets, including Yeats, to a study of the occult. AE was also a painter, and though Alfred had not seen the canvasses which portrayed the vision of Faeryland, he knew AE's verse:

We hold the Ireland in the heart
More than the land our eyes have seen
And love the goal for which we start

More than the tale of what has been . . .
We would no Irish sign efface,
But yet our lips would gladlier hail
The first-born of the Coming Race
Than the last splendour of the Gael.
No blazoned banner we unfold —
One charge alone we give to youth
Against the sceptred myth to hold
The golden heresy of truth.

Although his vision was mystical AE was also a tireless orga-
nizer for the agricultural co-operative movement, and Alfred was
certainly aware of this more political side of his character.

In the Willmore household the outbreak of rebellion in
Dublin in 1916 stirred tense excitement, especially after the
execution of the leaders. Christine, having escaped from the
clutches of the Beast, Aleister Crowley, now became obsessed
with Irish nationalism; the Proclamation of the Republic set her
mind afire. Their father, like most businessmen even in Ireland,
talked of the young hotheads, of a German plot and of it being
a stab in the back of Great Britain. Their mother declared that
the whole world seemed to have gone mad. Peg, usually nicknamed "Scatty", surprised everybody by thinking it wonderful
that "a little handful of men" should have stood up against
"the greatest power in the world to take what their conquerors
would not give them". This provided Christine's cue as she
declaimed:

"Pearse has said it all: 'It is Easter Monday! Christ has
risen from the tomb! Ireland has risen from slavery'."[3]

Alfred agreed at first with Peg and Christine but switched
the discussion to McMaster:

"I wonder what Mac thinks about it all? . . . He's back in
Ireland now, you know."

"Yes, but he's not in Dublin, thank God," Maimie [Mar-
jorie] assured him. "I'd a letter from him yesterday, he's
touring with a little theatre company, he's in Westport in
County Mayo."

"Now there's a lovely boy for you," Mother said. "And wasn't he very wise to get out of London before conscription came in, for everyone says it's coming in now?"[4]

The peaceful suburb of Willesden was no more immune than any other part of England to the war propaganda and jingoism which pervaded the country in the early years of the "Great War". His mother worried about conscription and her only son, consoling herself that her boy was "not old enough and won't be, please the good Lord, until this desperate old war'll be over". Marjorie, it appears, did not approve of her Anew running back to Ireland to tour the countryside "when so many men — Irish as well as English are risking their lives to win this war."[5] McMaster, the Irishman, would not have been eligible for conscription but the English-born Alfred would.

Turning his attention for the moment away from his art and his dreams of Ireland, Alfred made his debut as a juvenile lead in a rather slight comedy, *Felix Gets a Month*, which opened at the Haymarket Theatre on 6 February 1917. He was unhappy with his performance in what was described as "a sorry play"; he was not mentioned in *The Times* review and ruefully admitted that he was "often late for rehearsals and very bad in the part."[6]

With conscription looming and his thoughts more and more focused on Ireland and the Irish language, Alfred spoke of following Anew McMaster there. His mother, however, sounded a realistic note:

"And what'll you do anyway? No proper theatres — oh yes, the Abbey, I know, sure all they do there is old plays about tinkers and things, not your style at all I'd say."[7]

But neither were plays like *Felix Gets a Month* suited to his style, and his apparent dissatisfaction with the London stage in general no doubt contributed to his decision to leave for Ireland.

He left Euston station with Maire O'Keefe and her mother on the night mail train for Ireland on 26 March 1917. "Aunt Craven" went to escape the smog, to be with her delicate daughter, and to cosset Alfred. Whether worries about conscription motivated him or not, Alfred undoubtedly felt drawn to answer Yeats's romantic call to young artists to come to Ireland, "where the soul of man may be about to wed the soul of the earth."[8] In later years MacLiammóir gave the impression that it was to his homeland he had been drawn back:

> I then thought of Ireland not so much as a place but as a fragrance, almost forgotten, but after the Insurrection in Dublin, I knew that I was destined to return, feeling that I could not stay in England any longer.[9]

Alfred Willmore was not unique in his belief that Ireland was a land apart, a place where he could recreate himself. A number of people born in Britain, some but not all with Irish connections, had become imbued with the separatist ideas which Yeats had embraced under the influence of the old Fenian, John O'Leary. Tom Clarke, the oldest of those executed for their parts in the 1916 Rising, was born on the Isle of Wight. His comrade-in-arms James Connolly, the socialist leader of the Irish Citizen Army, never made known the place of his birth, which was in fact Edinburgh. James Larkin, the labour leader, had been born in Liverpool. Even before the 1916 Rising, Sir Roger Casement had abandoned the British Consular Service to import arms from Germany to aid an Irish rebellion. Erskine Childers, who had fought with the British Army in the Boer War and had been Clerk to the House of Commons, also brought in guns for the republicans.

In the cultural field there was a similar movement from Britain to Ireland after 1916 and during the twenties. Dr Robin Flower from Oxford, and the Greek scholar and Marxist, George Thompson (who had like Alfred attended Gaelic League classes in London), played important roles in the emergence of a literature in Irish in the remote Blasket Islands. Sir Arnold Bax, Master of the King's Music, contributed to the literary movement under the pseudonym of Dermot O'Byrne. Even Maud Gonne, the contemporary Cathleen Ni Houlihan, embodiment of the spirit of nationhood, was English.

When he arrived in Ireland, Alfred Willmore spent his first fortnight in a kind of spiritual quarantine, outside yet within view of Dublin, at Kingstown (now Dún Laoghaire) — "a dull remorselessly suburban place with its row after row of consequential shops, its orgy of trams, its high, forbidding walls". He and Máire looked longingly across the bay at Howth Head, which he had visited with Marjorie in 1913 when he had played in *Peter Pan* at the Theatre Royal. After Kingstown they spent several months at Stansfield House on Strand Road in Sandymount, but Alfred contracted typhoid fever and had to be removed to Cork Street Fever Hospital. After his recovery he was visited by Marjorie — who may also have come in search of Anew McMaster, still on tour in "the bacon and cabbages", as he called the provinces. Peg, too, visited with her new husband, bearing the very English, very unromantic name of Higginbottom.

It was the spring of 1918 before Máire and Alfred reached their Land of Heart's Desire. Aunt Craven had found a cottage in Howth; it stood at the top of the village and a *boithrín*, or track, led up from it to the Head and the cave under the cliffs where the legendary Diarmuid and Gráinne had hidden from the pursuit of Fionn MacCumhaill. Despite many wanderings, Howth was to be home for Aunt Craven and MacLiammóir for many of the years ahead.

The move to the cottage, named Loughoreen (*Loch a' Raoin*, the Lake of the Uplands) coincided with the choice of a name suitable for an Irish artist. Alfred was so utterly English that it could not possibly be allowed to survive the passage from London to Dublin, from Englishness to Irishness. Alfred the Great, in history the unifying monarch, in legend a potent figure, Alfred of the cakes; Alfred, too, not just of legend but also Alfred Lord Tennyson. His family nickname was Mickie, after his role in *Peter Pan*, so it may have seemed but a short step to settle upon the name Micheál. There may have been other reasons, other considerations behind the eventual choice, but whatever they may have been, Alfred was let slip into the wash of the past and Micheál stepped into the future. As to his surname, he simply invented an Irish version of Willmore and settled, after some trial and error, on MacLiammóir, a name never seen before but a name, nonetheless, which would pass muster. His earliest watercolours were variously signed Micheál Willmore, Micheál MacUaillmóir, or simply initialled M. MacU. His earliest essays and stories — all in Irish and published in periodicals from 1917 onwards — were usually signed Mac-Liammhóir. This spelling approximates to the pronunciation of his name by Irish speakers like Piaras Béaslaí who knew him in those years. The eventual retention of the double "m" without an aspirate may have puzzled philolo-gists but its uniqueness no doubt appealed to him.

His first published article, *"Politidheacht"* (Politics), appeared in the Gaelic League weekly, *An Claidheamh Soluis*, on 1 December 1917 under the unsightly surname MacUaim-mhóir. It was written in reply to an earlier contribution by Micheál Ó Conláin which asserted that the language revival movement should be independent of politics. MacLiammóir politely disagreed, taking the view common amongst the younger generation that political progress should go hand in hand with the spread of Irish as a spoken language. This was a contentious stance: when the unity and independence of the country had been adopted as one of the Gaelic League's objectives in 1915, Douglas Hyde, a founding member of the organization, had resigned in protest. But "If our leaders have no Irish," wrote MacLiammóir, "there is little hope for the language. We will still be painting (*sic*) and growing spuds for England."

In a letter to the editor of *Fáinne an Lae* (the successor to *An Claidheamh Soluis*) in the issue of 30 March 1918, he made a plea for drama in the Irish language: "The production of new plays in Irish, especially in Dublin, would help greatly; such presentations should be seen not only in halls and parochial centres but in the principal theatres." Clearly referring to the Abbey Theatre he continued: "If a certain national theatre that we already have in Dublin were to do a play in Irish once a month, it would be a great assistance to the language". He added that "there are already a small number of good plays available in Irish". It was certainly remarkable that this comparatively recent student of Irish had acquired the competence and confidence to tackle such issues in the leading periodical published in Irish in those turbulent years.

MacLiammóir's first patron in Dublin was Joseph Holloway, the somewhat eccentric Dublin architect who designed the original Abbey Theatre for Miss Annie Frederika Horniman in 1904. An inveterate first-nighter and diarist, Holloway became the Samuel Pepys of the Irish theatre, recording his impressions of nearly every first night in Dublin for the best part of fifty years. When he died in 1944, two hundred and twenty volumes of his manuscript notes were deposited in the National Library. He was also an insatiable collector of paintings and drawings of theatrical interest. When MacLiammóir visited Holloway at his home in Haddington Road, with an introduction from the former Abbey actress Una O'Connor, he noticed that the walls were "smothered with pictures". Before he left he had added three more, line and wash drawings, at a price of six guineas. This seemed a princely sum compared to his weekly salary in the West End "where he was murdered eight times weekly in *Macbeth*" for two pounds and ten shillings.

In the Green Room of the theatre, Holloway introduced him to the Abbey players. In their presence and manner none of them were like the actors he had known, "resembling more the members of his own family". Maureen Delany mothered him and Arthur Shields, Eric Gorman and Dorothy Lynd bought a few more of the watercolours. MacLiammóir became good friends with Shields; they were both interested in the theatre and in cultural nationalism. Shields, generally called "Boss", was a brother of Barry Fitzgerald, at that time a civil servant and part-time actor before his O'Casey roles made him famous. "Boss" Shields had been one of the few Protestants who had fought in Easter Week and he had been imprisoned for a time in Frongoch prison camp in Wales. MacLiammóir makes clear, however, that Shields was now opposed to physical force methods. Another Abbey acquaintance was the secretary of the company, Charles Millington. They introduced MacLiammóir to the brilliant French scholar and critic A.J. (Con) Leventhal.

Late one night this quartet joined in a seance in the Abbey Green Room, a more likely venue for card playing. MacLiammóir, having learned something of spiritualism from Christine and his reading of Yeats, directed operations. The four sat in a circle in the dim light of a gasfire, hands joined in expectation of a message from the spirit world. MacLiammóir sensed some mediumistic traits in Leventhal. Leventhal appeared to enter a trance and the three others saw his features disappear until his face become "a wall of flesh". Though they received no message they were startled and switched on the light. Leventhal's features returned to normal as he awoke from the trance. Millington, who was quite scared, told MacLiammóir "that he should not tinker with the unknown". Máire O'Keefe, too, felt that there should be no more seances at the Abbey.[10]

With a foot in the door of the theatre, MacLiammóir was given the small part of a crippled boy in a new play, *Blight*, billed as by "Alpha and Omega". It was mainly the work of Dr Oliver St John Gogarty with some assistance from a friend, a Dublin lawyer named Joseph O'Connor. It was one of the earliest of the Abbey plays set in a Dublin tenement and drew largely on Gogarty's experience as a medical student in the disease-ridden slums. But for MacLiammóir the seance seems to have been a more noteworthy performance; years later he told Ulick O'Connor that he was literally bored stiff, having to lie still at the end of a bed with scarcely a line to say for most of the play.

About this time he got to know a fellow writer in Irish, also a refugee from London, a rapscallion of genius, Sean Phádraic Ó Conaire. It was under the influence of Ó Conaire and his fondness for the drop that MacLiammóir changed to Connaught Irish and whiskey. One of the most humorous stories in *All for Hecuba* tells of an escapade with Ó Conaire at the first night of Daniel Corkery's *The Labour Leader* at the Abbey. The house was packed and the pair were given seats in the wings where they saw the play through an alcoholic haze. Towards the end of the third act, Ó Conaire became obstreperous and crawled on his hands and knees through the open fireplace onto the set bellowing, "*Go mbeannaighe Dia isteach annseo*" (God save all here), just as the final curtain fortunately fell. At the curtain-call Arthur Shields apologized for the absence of the author, but Ó Conaire would have none of it and doffed his hat and bowed low in an attempt to convey to the audience that he was the author or his deputy. In MacLiammóir's words "it was a highly successful but outrageous performance", but hardly one that would have endeared Ó Conaire or himself to their Abbey associates.

In September 1918 MacLiammóir played in the Hardwicke Street production of John Galsworthy's light comedy, *Joy*. It was a semi-professional presentation in which several Abbey players such as Barry Fitzgerald and Irene Kelly took part. This *ad hoc* company had no licence to perform the play and no money was taken on the opening night. According to the *Evening Telegraph*, "the audience displayed a cordial sympathy with the two young actresses (Dorothy Lynd and Irene Kelly), and made allowances for the blemishes". The actor who played Dick Merton, Joy's lover, was variously named in reviews as MacUaimmhóir, MacMinhóir and Michael Maguire. Holloway in his diary identified the actor as Michael Willmore who "though awkward and ungainly in his movements — almost got me interested near the end by the youthful exuberance of his manner in wooing Joy". Evidently MacLiammóir had yet to make his mark as an actor, having failed to get the critics to spell his name correctly when they mentioned him at all.

MacLiammóir's first attempt at stage design was for Edward Martyn's play, *Regina Eyre*, produced by the Irish Theatre Company in the forbidding and uncomfortable Hardwicke Hall in 1919. A wealthy Galway landowner and patron of the arts, Martyn was a fervent Ibsenite who tried to interest

Dublin audiences in the Continental drama of ideas, as distinct from the peasant plays seen at the Abbey. MacLiammóir designed some steep rocks against an azure sky on the tiny stage. These were to represent Carrantuohill, the highest mountain in Ireland, which two benighted actresses were expected to climb. "Apparently the idea is," surmised the *Evening Telegraph*, "that only a mountaineer with a clear conscience could accomplish the feat. Quite right, too, because Regina goes up and up and up and comes down unscathed, but Dymphna topples over the precipice and ends the annoyance of the playwright, the dramatis personae and the audience." [11]

Likewise, Joseph Holloway was not impressed by the design for *Regina Eyre*: "There was a long delay between Acts 3 and 4 to make ready the mountain-top scene which seemed to consist of impossible rocks (I believe Michael Williams (*sic*) was the artist) against an azure sky. Here all the characters assembled and spoke a lot about cleansing their souls on mountain tops." [12]

Of the Hardwicke Street Theatre, MacLiammóir recalled:
The stage was inadequate. I acted there once, and on another occasion painted a moutainside set for one of Martyn's own symbolic plays — a gaunt Ibsenic affair — in which Máire Nic Shiúbhlaigh performed. . . . The seating was haphazard in arrangement and uncompromising as to carnal comfort (one pushed chairs about in the front rows and sat on baskets, as I remember, in the back). Even the lighting was of the sad and glacial quality one associates with political meetings of an intimate and conspiratorial kind. . . . The settings, except when Martyn got going on one for his mountain-side were, as well as I remember, mainly curtains. [13]

Outside of the theatre, MacLiammóir had become known for his drawings and received some commissions as a book illustrator for the Talbot Press. He provided the cover illustration for the published text of *Finn Varra Maa — An Irish Fairy Pantomime* by T. H. Nally, produced in December 1917 at the Theatre Royal. Among the collections of stories he illustrated were Seumus O'Kelly's *Waysiders* and Daniel Corkery's *A*

Munster Twilight. While his drawings show the influence of Jack B. Yeats, MacLiammóir, with unaccustomed smugness, commented that "these illustrations were enthusiastically received by the newspapers, sometimes more enthusiastically than the stories themselves, which naturally irritated the authors".[14] Encouraged by the landscape painter Paul Henry, MacLiammóir had a one-man exhibition in 1919 under the title "Fantasies in Colour" which was highly praised by AE in the *Irish Statesman.* Many of the watercolours — fantasies of nude fairies encircling snowy-coloured hills or wee folk trooping over mountains on moonlit nights — show touches of Arthur Rackham and Harry Clarke. In An Fód Mona, a literary cafe, MacLiammóir was known more as a painter than an actor; Francis Stuart remembers him as "very good-looking but effeminate".

MacLiammóir also frequented 6 Harcourt Street where he went with Máire to join Sinn Féin and attend weekly meetings at which they heard ardent speeches, ferocious arguments and confident plans for Ireland's future. He canvassed for Sinn Féin candidate Dick Mulcahy in the 1918 election, only to be shown the door of Mespil House by the formidable hostess and artist Sarah Purser. Ever resourceful, he went to the servants' entrance where he got the votes of the staff. Mulcahy was elected deputy to the first Dáil Eireann. MacLiammóir's political activism did not go unnoticed: the cottage at Howth was searched by the Black and Tans. His Gaelic League and Sinn Féin cards were deciphered as "something suspicious in that bleeding lingo", but no arrests were made.

His mother visited Howth in the summer of 1918; it was the last time MacLiammóir would see her, as she died a few months later. He did not attend her funeral in London, merely mentioning laconically that there was not enough money to bring her body home "to be buried in Irish ground". This apparent indifference to her death was not an isolated example of his separation and alienation from his family in England. Indeed, as the creation of his Irish identity proceeded so too did he progressively consign the Lees and the Willmores and their forebears from London to an ever dimmer and more distant past.

When Aunt Craven's sister, Hilda, visited Howth in 1919 there were some tensions when she insisted on going around on Armistice Day plastered with Union Jacks and poppies. Craven saw this as provocation but she probably overestimated the number of Sinn Féiners in Howth in those days. A more welcome visitor to Howth was the irrepressible Anew McMaster with his hilarious descriptions of touring the fit-ups:

"Tired to death of it all, darlings. . . . *Terrible* melodramas like *No Mother to Guide Her* and *Waifs and Strays of Erin's Isle* dear, terrible digs, all Sacred Heart pictures and fleas in the beds, *terrible* actors: so bad some of them that even the *audiences* are beginning to notice."[15]

To Micheál and Máire, the terror of the political war being waged around them seemed to recede as they lit fires on the Hill of Howth at the Festivals of *Samhain*, *Lá Fhéile Bhríde*, *Bealtaine* and *Lúnasa* in celebration of the *sidhe* and the Ancient Gods. Soon curfew and the possibility of more Black and Tan raids reawakened in him grim memories of the recent past. He had come to share Arthur Shields' distrust of revolutionary activity and violence but remained firm in his resolve to serve Ireland as an artist. It was not easy, however, to live up to Yeats's exhortation:

I would have Ireland recreate the ancient arts . . . as they were understood when they moved a whole people and not a few people who have grown up in a leisured class and made this understanding their business.[16]

The great influenza epidemic and the ravages of tuberculosis tempered MacLiammóir's and his friends' youthful enthusiasm. Máire was struck down by consumption, the white plague of Ireland. She was fortunate that she could go in 1920 to a cure-resort at Davos — Thomas Mann's Magic Mountain — in Switzerland. Her mother went with her, of course, and Micheál felt compelled to follow this friend from the distant past, the girl whose best feature was her "up-slanting luminous, blue-green eyes". He seemed in thrall to a sphinx, a *spéirbhean* who could assist in the imaginative recreation of himself.

· III ·

The Magic Mountain

There is something terribly morbid in the modern sympathy with pain. One should sympathize with the colour, the beauty, the joy of life.

Oscar Wilde

MACLIAMMÓIR REVELLED IN the dazzling sun and snow of Davos before setting out on what seems like a Grand Tour of Europe. Although never less than a devoted companion to Máire, this carefree existence with several new friends allowed him freedom to express his preference for his own sex in a manner which would have been unacceptable, if not impossible, during his four years in Dublin. Now there were exciting trips to Venice, Florence, Rome and Paris with an American, Robert, whose attitude to sex was entertainingly ambivalent.

Máire warned him against "falling in love" with a true friend, Jack Dunne from Kildare, as he was unlikely to respond; "I do not want you to be hurt," she added. She was proved right; Micheál admitted hurt. Then a patient at Davos, Jack Dunne nevertheless became a lifelong friend.

He kept a diary in Irish and wrote in a large, sprawling hand late at night rough notes for future publications. The captions to the photographs in his album covering this period he also wrote in Irish. He had brief encounters with Russians, Germans, Scandinavians and Americans of both sexes, and amongst the photographs are several of MacLiammóir with handsome young men whom he identified only by first names or pseudonyms both in the album and in *Enter a Goldfish*.

One of the talented, artistic young men who influenced MacLiammóir during his wanderings through Western Europe was Hubert Duncombe, who shared MacLiammóir's passion for ballet, particularly the Ballet Russe at Monte Carlo. Duncombe later worked as an actor at the Dublin Gate and with the well-known Irish director of the Cambridge Festival Theatre, Terence Gray, who wrote his obituary when he committed suicide in 1931:

> He was a man of intellectual attainment for he could speak fluently four European languages. . . . He was a quiet man with charming manners, on friendly terms with us all but intimate with none; his relations with the management were unmarred by dispute of any kind.[1]

For MacLiammóir these travels in Europe were the days of wine and roses. He created an air of mystery about this period; nothing so mundane as money was ever mentioned, nor was there any indication of how he earned a living apart from the sale of some paintings or illustrations. Aunt Craven and Máire had allowances from Máire's father and a wealthy and elderly cousin, Walter A. Dickey, appropriately nicknamed "Wad", entertained Micheál in Paris.

He continued to write for Irish periodicals — descriptive pieces of the Alps and Sicily with no references to his personal affairs. An exception is a manuscript draft of what was probably his first attempt to write a short story. It is entitled *"Cuimhne"* (Memory), just as one of his earliest watercolours was titled *An Chéad Chuimhne*. The short story or dream fragment tells of a man, dying in hospital from a gunshot wound, who in delirium believes he is back at school with a room-mate, Eoghan Ó Conaire. The patient is agitated because Eoghan's bed is missing. A baffled doctor sends for a priest he knows who is also named Eoghan Ó Conaire. The priest reveals that the hospital had previously been a boarding school and recalls the room he once shared with the dying man. Spiritual comfort or absolution is not mentioned, only hints at a dark secret shared long ago.

This obviously early effort must have been the first attempt in Irish to deal, albeit clumsily, with sexual adolescence. A more polished but less explicit version of this story appeared in 1929 under the title *"An Créacht"* (The Wound) in *Lá agus Óidhche*, a collection of essays and stories published by *An Gúm*, the Government Publications Office.

His first contribution to *An Sguab*, also reprinted in *Lá agus Óidhche*, was an account of a visit to Oberammergau in the Bavarian Alps in December 1922. The story of Oberammergau and its eight-hour performance of the Gospel story, from the entry of Christ into Jerusalem to the Resurrection on the third day after the Crucifixion, made a deep impression on MacLiammóir:

To my mind the most beautiful and moving scene was the first appearance of Christ, as he rode through the city in triumph to the acclamation of great crowds waving palms. I shall never forget my first view of him, on the donkey's back, in a white robe with a cloak of scarlet; the deep-set eyes; the arms outstretched in benediction, the mysterious smile on his lips. . . these things must be seen to be believed. . . . A ray of sunlight fell on him as he entered between the dark arches at the back of the stage, so that his head and shoulders were enveloped in a golden fire. Such sights are seen through a mist of tears, but at the same time, they betoken joy and exaltation. Anton Lang! he is not without fault as an actor . . . but where is the actor who could portray Christ or reveal him adequately to an audience — but his first entrance was really a miracle. I look back on it as one of the world's great works of art, taking its place beside the *Mona Lisa*, the statue of Apollo Belvidere, and the music of *Tristan and Isolde*. And Guido Mair, the actor who played Judas, is an artist of tremendous power. He portrayed the character of Judas with ready artistry down to the smallest detail; the yellow robe, the shrewd, wrinkled face, greed and fear glinting alternatively in his looks. It is hard to believe that both of these men have little experience of the actor's craft.[2]

For MacLiammóir, the depiction of the Last Supper invited comparison with Leonardo da Vinci's fresco in the Monastery of Maria della Grazie in Milan. The trial, crucifixion and resurrection, he concluded, brought the marathon performance to an ecstatic close. MacLiammóir made no mention or suggestion of an anti-semitic note in the presentation which, in later years, aroused controversy. Everything in Oberammergau was a wonder which brought him nearer to the heart of the mystery. Although never a churchgoer, MacLiammóir was always attracted by ceremonial and religious ritual.

MacLiammóir's first book, *Óidhcheannta Sidhe* (Faery Nights), a bilingual collection of four fairy stories for children, with his own illustrations in black and white, was published by the Talbot Press in 1922. The stories dealt with the ancient festivals of *Bealtaine*, *Lúnasa*, *Samhain* and *Lá 'le Bríde*, and had an English translation on alternate pages. An attractive little book, it was reprinted in 1988. The May Eve story was later adapted by him into a play in Irish, *Óidhche Bealtaine*, and published in a series of plays for children by *An Gúm*. He also wrote a short sketch in Irish, *Lúlú*, about a lady and her pet dog. Along with his stories for children and his contributions in Irish to periodicals published in Dublin, MacLiammóir had a vague ambition to write, on a suggestion by Máire O'Keefe, a full-length play in Irish.

The play was to be based on the best-known of all the *Fianna* sagas: Gráinne, the daughter of the High King of Ireland was bethrothed to Fionn MacCumhaill, the ageing leader of the *Fianna*, a group of warriors famous in Irish mythology. On the night of the betrothal, Gráinne eloped from Tara with a youthful warrior, Diarmuid, who had a love-spot (*ball seirce*) on his forehead on which no woman could gaze without falling in love with him. Despite Gráinne's wiles, Diarmuid remained faithful to Fionn, having sworn never to be her lover. As a symbol of this fidelity, he left unbroken bread wherever they spent the night. For seven years they were pursued by Fionn and his warriors, across the length and breath of Ireland, and the places where they hid may be pointed out to this day — Beann Eadair (Howth), Dubhros (Durrus) and Ben Bulben where Diarmuid was mortally wounded when, like Adonis, he fought a mythical wild boar. Fionn could save him with a magic potion but Diarmuid was left to die, so that Fionn could at last take Gráinne to his bed.

The dark ironic ending of the tale contrasts sharply with the common folk-tales of the beautiful young princess who, being forced to marry an old king, elopes with a young prince. Both Máire and Micheál felt drawn to this story and its bitter irony. Máire felt that she understood the mind of Gráinne, while Micheál identified with Diarmuid who, in Tom Moore's words, "was never tempted by woman or gold". The play was so long in the making that it was never staged in Máire's lifetime but MacLiammóir dedicated the published text to his *anamchara* (soul companion) who had inspired him to write it.

In 1924 he returned to Ireland to appear in an Irish-made film, *Land of Her Fathers*, playing opposite Phyllis Wakely, a Trinity College student and amateur actress. Among the Abbey actors in the cast were Maureen Delany, Eileen Crowe and M.J. Bolan. Scripted by Dorothea Byrne, wife of the novelist Donn Byrne, and produced by John Hurley, the only complete copy of the film was stolen in New York and cannot be traced.

In August 1924 MacLiammóir's first short story in English was published in the prestigious *Dublin Magazine*. Entitled "Transference", it was based on an experience at the ballet in Paris. Later that year he went to Naples to meet Anew McMaster on his return from a long tour of Australia where he had been playing leading roles with Oscar Asche. McMaster soon returned to the West End in London, where he acted with Gladys Cooper.

In 1925 MacLiammóir, Máire and Aunt Craven returned from their European rambles to the quieter life that awaited them back in Howth. His adventurous times of travelling and enjoying brief raptures in often exotic circumstances were behind him now and he settled into the comparative repose of life overlooking Dublin Bay and the Irish Sea. In the same year in London his sister Marjorie, much to MacLiammóir's surprise, married his great friend and exemplar, Anew McMaster.

The newly-weds visited Howth in the summer of 1926, finding Micheál and Máire in somewhat melancholy mood, for Maire's health had not improved. MacLiammóir's other friends came and went but his friendship with Máire seemed unending. Aunt Craven, Micheál and Máire travelled to Mentone for the winter. Micheál went from there to Davos to see the American, Robert, who had had to return there on doctor's orders. After a week Micheál came back to Mentone to spend Christmas with Máire. She developed pneumonia, but they celebrated the New Year with champagne, believing the crisis was over.

Máire relapsed and the six days and nights to *Nollaig na mBan* — Little Christmas — went by hideously. The friends of a million years, as Máire said, were to part in silence. On the morning of 7 January 1927, Máire died slowly. "Máire could not lose consciousness until the last moment," wrote MacLiammóir, "and it was clear from her eyes that she heard the death-rattle in her own throat."[3]

No death had brought such anguish to MacLiammóir, a pain which lingered longer as a result of the delays in bringing Máire's remains back to Ireland. She had wished to be cremated and to have her ashes scattered on the summit of Howth Head. As the coffin was being sent — to Marseilles — for cremation, Micheál placed a copy of Yeats's poems between her crossed hands. The casket of ashes was to be kept until May Eve, the Feast of *Bealtaine*, for the final ritual at Howth, which had become for them the Magic Mountain.

To blur the hard reality MacLiammóir wrote to Anew McMaster, who now had his own company on tour in England, to tell him of his desire "to learn to act again":

My Dear Mac,

Now that Máire is no more I find it impossible to go on with the old life. Tree used to think I could act and gave me all the boys' parts he could find for me at His Majesty's. You were of the same opinion, or you said you were. Could you give me any work? I've forgotten much and feel in a worse condition than a real beginner because I'm conscious of the depths beneath my feet. But if you could give me bits like Rosencrantz and Montano for a bit. . . . Where are you? Write to Paris and tell me when I can come. I saw Noel [Coward] and Ivor [Novello] at the Ballet in Monte Carlo the other day and they sent their love. I think they look so well and happy because they have definite things to do. It is impossible to paint, hoping vaguely to do something terrific; to write plays, wondering will they be ever produced. By the way, the play I'm doing for you has stuck, but maybe someday . . . I suppose *Diarmuid and Gráinne* is the only title. People in Ireland will know who one means anyway. If I ever finish it . . . I'm writing it in Irish — it goes better that way, but I am translating it scene by scene for you.

One must be forced from the outside sometimes to do things, and in the profession the curtain goes up at eight and the show goes on no matter what mood one is in. That's how I hope to find salvation.[4]

The McMaster company had toured the Irish and English provinces in 1926, and in the spring of 1927 MacLiammóir joined them in Canterbury. His parts were somewhat better than he had hoped, and included Lorenzo in the *Merchant of Venice* and Cassio in *Othello*. His initiation as a twenty-seven-year-old juvenile lead in Shakespeare was not easy although McMaster, "as reliable in all theatre affairs as he was outrageous outside them", did his best to make him forget *Oliver Twist* and the boyish charm:

I set myself to the learning of these lines, muttering them to myself in buses and tubes but I had lost the knack, the intense yet lightly held concentration, the elasticity, as of a metal bow and arrow with which one absorbs a part, and I found that I was no longer learning automatically at rehearsal which habit I had acquired when I was a child. It was a question now of flogging the unwilling and unruly brain, that wandering lunatic in my head that is always waiting for an escape from the present moment into those dim and fiery coloured regions, those starry hollows in the imagination and the memory where, undisturbed by conscience or the need for action one can fulfil every dream.[5]

Hard as it was to play Shakespeare convincingly, he was even less at ease in modern plays which McMaster included in the repertoire to ensure a good box-office take. And he was particularly glad not to be cast in a sentimental comedy called *Smilin' Tru'*, as this gave him the opportunity to fulfil a solemn promise.

On his night off he rushed to Dublin to be at Howth on May Eve when he would, as he had promised her, scatter Máire's ashes on Beann Eadair (Howth Head). But his expedition began to take on the elements of a farce when he found that he was unable to open the casket containing the ashes. He hid the casket under a furze bush near the cairn on the summit, but the conductor of the Howth tram reported this seemingly suspicious behaviour to the Gárda Síochána, who took possession of the casket. Cremation was not then legal in Ireland and he was charged — under the name Michael Wilmore (*sic*) — with an offence under the Cemeteries Bye-Laws. The charge was dismissed when it came before the District Court and on the May Eve of the following year he retrieved the casket from Howth Barracks and finally succeeded in fulfilling Máire's last wishes.

After his hurried rush to Howth on his first, abortive funeral mission, he was back the next day in Woking, tired and exhausted but able to play Laertes in *Hamlet* creditably.

As they toured McMaster continued to needle and wheedle Micheál to greater heights. His direction was both forthright and practical:

"Your voice is like a rather beautiful fog-horn . . . but you can do more with it than that. Use some top notes as well. And kindly don't take a drink before the show is over. Ever." [6]

Not even McMaster, who played all the leading parts, was quite satisfied with the provincial tour in England. He was of the opinion that, outside of London, the English did not really like Shakespeare. At Tunbridge Wells, after a row with his leading lady, McMaster decided to go back to Ireland. The change of plan was much to MacLiammóir's and Marjorie's liking, but some of the English members of the company thought it preposterous and declined to travel. One of the leading actors defected at the last moment and McMaster had to stay in London to try to get an actor who was not only good enough to play Iago, Claudius and Macduff in Shakespeare and Taffy in *Trilby*, but who was also willing to tour the fit-ups in Ireland. He succeeded in finding one, even if he was "bloody expensive". Also among those who agreed to join the Irish tour was a young and striking actress, Coralie Carmichael. Born in London, of Scottish extraction, she had played with the Birmingham Repertory Company and at the Court Theatre. A tall, statuesque woman of vivacious personality, she had the versatility to switch from tragedy to comedy — an essential quality for a repertory actress.

The huddle of players left Paddington Station for Rosslare, and arrived in an Ireland that neither knew nor cared about the dreams and ambitions of actors. It was the year of the murder of the Minister for Justice, Kevin O'Higgins, and of the Fianna Fáil party's decision to enter the Dáil under the leadership of Eamon de Valera. Yet McMaster, getting ready to tour the length and breath of a troubled and impoverished land, was blissfully unaware that those little towns existed for anything but to allow him play Shakespeare. And for MacLiammóir, longing to live there as an actor and artist, Ireland was not just a place but a stage.

· IV ·

Not Only Gaelic, But Free!

We Irish are accused eternally of brooding over the images of the past, but in reality it is by the future, more it may be than other people in the world, that we are driven. It is for the vision of a most questionable posterity that we walk out from our homes, that we dream and plot and play the fool, that we suffer and die. We have created a past for ourselves that we may the more clearly see the future of our hearts' desire, and in the continual striving and sacrifice offered up for that future lies perhaps the only Irish virtue.

Micheál MacLiammóir *All for Hecuba*

THE PARTICLES OF chalk that danced in the sunlight pouring through the open schoolhouse door were scattered by the swagger of his entry. A flashy young man in black corduroys, wearing a red kerchief, swept a sombrero from his head. He took the teacher and pupils by surprise with his salutation.

"*Go mbeannaí Dia dhíbh! Lig dom mé féin a chur in aithne dhíbh, a bhuachaillí is a mháistir. MacLiammóir m'ainmse.* Micheál MacLiammóir," he continued in an uninterrupted flow, "I'm an actor with Anew McMaster's Shakespearean Company who will give a matinée performance of *The Merchant of Venice* at three o'clock tomorrow and I have come to ask your teacher here to let you free of class to attend. Admission sixpence for pupils and ninepence for any of your parents or older brothers and sisters who would like to come."

It was my first sight of an actor at close quarters. He seemed from a world far away from that small town in Clare. He was different, not in the least like the foreigners who came for the fishing or the knickerbockered engineers who had come from Germany to install turbines for the Shannon Electrical Scheme. If it had been a girl, I'd have sworn he was wearing rouge. He sounded all the more exciting and mystifying in Irish — even the teacher was taken aback by such fluency from a play-actor, a breed generally regarded as of obscure origin like gipsies and Indian pedlars. And as it was near the summer holidays and those who did not fancy Shakespeare could save hay, the teacher nodded his assent: "*Tá go maith, a dhuine uasail*".

It was a good stroke by McMaster to have Micheál visit the schools in Killaloe. His command of Irish was bound to impress the teachers who in those days were not quite fluent in the language themselves. Another of McMaster's publicity promotions was to get as many of his company as possible to go to Mass or the Protestant service on Sundays; when business was particularly poor, McMaster was reputed to have attended both services on the same Sunday. And finally there was the town crier — a bellman who paraded the streets hollering

"Town Hall Tonight. Anew McMaster and his famous Shakespearean Company direct from the Theatre Royal present *Hamlet* in Five Acts to be followed by a raffle and a laughable farce." This was not quite correct, because there was in fact no farce, but the crier could not be expected to change his customary spiel for a minor detail.

We students in fifth class were expected to do anything that might further our education, so we were marched to the hall in single file for our first taste of Shakespeare. I cannot say whether MacLiammóir played Lorenzo or Bassanio for none of the actors wore black corduroys or spoke Irish and all of them wore rouge on stage. There were no programmes and, even if there had been, our spare coppers were needed for sweets or the raffle. The play was shortened for the matinée; some scenes were cut, either to avoid doubling or to make the story-line clearer for the young audience. On a couple of occasions McMaster came before the front curtain to explain the intricacies of the plot to us schoolchildren who did not really get the hang of it until the courtroom scene between Portia and Shylock. Then things took a turn for the worse in our eyes for, after all the sharpening of the knife, it was a deep disappointment to us that Shylock did not carve his pound of flesh straight from Antonio's bosom. But bloodthirsty though we undoubtedly were, it gave MacLiammóir a particular pleasure to play to audiences such as we provided, and he wrote in his diary about another matinée of *The Merchant of Venice*:

Malta. 11 May 1956. Special Matinée for school children of the *Merchant*. This oddly enough glorious; the best audience for Shakespeare outside some remote country town in the West of Ireland, that one can imagine, for the canker of an academic half-understanding of the Master had not yet corrupted their minds: they have no knowledge of him whatsoever, and they are the very people for whom he wrote.

When Bassanio guessed rightly about the leaden casket they frenziedly applauded; when Portia put Shylock into a hole about the pound of flesh they rose to their feet loudly

screaming: when Salerio (or is it now Salerino?) came with
the news about the wreck of Antonio's ships they listened in
silence as stricken as though they were hearing the story of
their own ruin. None of them seemed to know what fate was
in store for any of the people on the stage, or what perils or
triumphs were to be revealed, and this is the only way to
enjoy the *Merchant* and any of those plays of his that are one
degree less in stature than the greatest works. The pleasure
of ignorance is not, perhaps, as complete as that of knowledge, but ignorance has moments, as it had to-day, as lovely
as young hair blown in a frolic wind straight from Parnassus.[1]

The pleasures of ignorance: they were there in plenty in
the Clare of the twenties! MacLiammóir and McMaster were
always appreciative of the response to Shakespeare in rural
Ireland, and, in return, some of us grew to appreciate McMaster
as we got older. McMaster used to quote an old countryman as
having told him that modern plays like *Trilby* and *Love from a
Stranger* were "too high falutin'" for his kind and that they
preferred *Oedipus Rex*! In the hungry twenties country people
were engrossed by the magic of theatre in much the same way
as the groundlings of Shakespeare's Globe in the years of the
First Elizabeth. Rural Ireland had its own Burbage in the person
of McMaster, the last of the great touring actor-managers who
played all the great Shakespearean parts until his death in
1962. MacLiammóir came in goodly company, and wrote
glowingly of places like Cappoquin, Dungarvan and Ennis,
where his first Irish tour with McMaster ended.

A new excitement had also come into his life: the man
whom McMaster had unearthed in London. "Much the best I
could find, dear," said McMaster. "Marvellous audition, bloody
expensive, can't be helped." A sturdily built young man in a
tweed cap and overcoat was introduced: "This is my brother-
in-law, Micheál MacLiammóir; this is our new Iago, Micheál,
Mr Hilton Edwards!"[2]

McMaster, did not, however, think this new actor and
Micheál would get on at all.

"He's so English dear," Mac cried, "and although his large nose and his sheer brilliance would make you think he was a Jew, it seems he's not one. Not that I'd object to him if he *was* one, dear, but I don't think he is. No, he's just a John Bull with the lid off, Britannia's son, and I'd be very surprised if I found you could tolerate him for five minutes." [3]

Hilton Edwards was one of the most experienced actors to tour Ireland in the twenties. Born in London on 2 February 1903, his mother's name was Murphy but he never claimed to be anything but an uncompromising Englishman. At the age of seventeen he joined the Charles Doran Shakespearean Company, which had as members such actors as Donald Wolfit and Ralph Richardson. He played with them in Dublin, Belfast and Cork in 1921. He became a member of the Old Vic Company the following year, and played under the direction of Robert Atkins in Shakespeare's plays and in *The School for Scandal* and Goethe's *Faust*. Possessing a fine baritone voice, he sang in the Angels' Chorus in a Christmas production of one of the Chester Nativity Plays. After a singing tour in South Africa he played a small part in *The Dybbuk*, a Jewish play about demonic possession, in the Royalty Theatre where he first worked with Peter Godfrey. Later Godfrey founded London's Gate Theatre in a ramshackle warehouse where he staged avant-garde Expressionist plays by George Kaiser and Ernst Toller. Edwards took part in some of these productions and was obviously impressed, not least by the title The Gate.

To McMaster's surprise, Edwards and MacLiammóir became inseparable friends. On St John's Eve they climbed Vinegar Hill outside Enniscorthy where the apparently unemotional Edwards and the mercurial MacLiammóir took part in the traditional ritual of leaping through the flames of the bonfire. Before the end of the summer Edwards contracted pneumonia and by the time he had recovered the tour had ended. Both Hilton and Micheál, who had stayed in Cork with the patient, were practically broke. To bolster their funds MacLiammóir had an exhibition of drawings at Gilbert's

Gallery in Cork and Edwards got a singing engagement at the Palace Theatre. A Dublin exhibition followed, while Edwards had singing dates at the Capitol and Corinthian cinemas where he appeared thrice daily during the intervals between films. When Edwards went on to his next dates in Derry, MacLiammóir travelled to London to bring Aunt Craven back to a new cottage she had found in Howth. For all but acting engagements he had almost completely severed his links with the country of his birth. The future now lay in Ireland.

He and his new partner talked endlessly about plans for a theatre in Ireland. They returned to the hard slog of another provincial tour with the inexhaustible McMaster, opening in Longford in the autumn of 1927. Life was not easy, playing at least eight performances most weeks in draughty halls with no dressing-rooms and corrugated roofs on which heavy rain beat a tattoo during the quietest scenes. At times they played on an improvised stage of long planks laid on trestles or empty porter barrels. In Cappoquin they played in a boathouse and were ferried from their "dressing-room" on the slip to the stage. As their theatrical fortunes ebbed and flowed, there were frequent rehearsals for new plays and new players. When McMaster got a fortnight's booking at the Abbey Theatre in December, the tide seemed to have turned.

Despite its successes on the road McMaster's company was not well known to Abbey theatregoers, but the critics were welcoming and they played to good houses. Holloway unaccustomedly arrived late to report in his diary:

Dec. 5: The night turned out wet. The Abbey, save the front seats, was thronged with an audience that followed Shakespeare's play with the keenest interest. I arrived just as "Hamlet" in the person of Anew McMaster, was almost (*sic*) to speak "To be or not to be" speech, and my eye saw a slim shapely figure clad in black with fine curly hair seated on a high back chair. He was speaking in somewhat measured or slow pace, in sweet toned musical voice and thoughtful way that seemed very human withal, and at once arrested my interest.

In the scene in the closet with his mother a great height of tragic grandeur was reached by both him and his queen mother, Esme Biddle, and the audience became enthusiastic after the scene and called the two players before the curtains — a compliment they richly deserved. The complete beauty of Miss Biddle's rich-dyed musical voice was slightly marred by a cold. She had a fine stage presence and acts with distinction. She and McMaster won the house from the start.

Michael Willmore (*sic*) made a picturesque looking "Laertes" and acted very well. . .I liked Coralie Carmichael's "Ophelia" and she was quite pathetic in her girlish madness. . . .

Dec.7: The last act of *Othello* was so finely played that it redeemed a rather uneven and unconvincing performance. In this act McMaster played with a wonderful power and restraint, and little Ann Clark made an ideal "Desdemona" . . . McMaster started his Othello rather unconvincingly in his speech to the Senate. It was not until his great scenes between him and "Iago" that he grew into the part and showed the fine player he undoubtedly is.

The "Iago" of Hilton Edwards wasn't quite satisfying; on the whole he spoke too rapidly for his words to be followed with clearness, and struck too many poses and tuppenny coloured attitudes . . . Michael Willmore was effective as "Montano" and J. C. Warren as "The Duke". Both "Iago" and "Othello" were twice called before the curtain after their great scene. This act ended in Othello's falling down in a fit and writhing on the floor. A fitting end to the whirlwind of passion that has gone before. . .⁴

Joseph Holloway's comments are particularly valuable for the little details he mentions — the custom of taking curtains, in operatic fashion, after big scenes; of Miss Biddle's cold (she usually kept a little bottle of whiskey in her handbag), and McMaster's "fit" after the jealousy scene, of which he was inordinately proud. "Did you know, Godfrey Tearle left out the fit," he told Harold Pinter years later, when Pinter toured with the company under the name David Baron. "He didn't do the fit. I'm older than Godfrey Tearle. But I do the fit. Don't I? At least I don't leave it out." [5]

Holloway, who had seen many great actors, had an eye for greatness in the making. His final summary of the season is remarkable for his prescience of McMaster's real potential:

Dec. 16: I have had a great feast of Shakespeare for the past fortnight and witnessed seven of the poet's works. The young actor, Anew McMaster, has proved himself a chip off the old block of great tragedians, and has made more than good as "Othello", "Hamlet" and "Romeo" — in fact, his "Othello" is a really remarkable achievement. Lawrence [W. J. Lawrence, a well-known critic and admirer of Bernard Shaw's favourite, the Shakespearean actor, Barry Sullivan] and I are of the opinion that he will bloom into the big tragic actor of his time. He has all the natural gifts that make a fine actor — height, good figure, handsome clearcut face, melodious voice of great range, and graceful gestures. He always pleases the eye as well as satisfies the mind. In *A Midsummer Night's Dream* his king of the fairies "Oberon" makes one think he was going for a beauty contest, he looked so imposing and handsome. He gave a dashing portrayal of "Petruchio" in *The Taming of the Shrew* and his "Macbeth" was vindictive and revengeful without a moment's relief. If he doesn't rise to the very top I, for one, shall be sorely disappointed. [6]

Even if McMaster never quite got the acclaim which he deserved, it must have been clear to MacLiammóir and Edwards that the leading roles would never be entrusted to them while McMaster was in charge. MacLiammóir was ambitious, though a little diffident after his long years of absence from the stage. Edwards, however, was at hand to pour flattery in his ear:

"Would you like a theatre of your own? I don't mean now, I don't mean for ages. But you won't be with Mac all your life. The day will come then you'll be ready for Romeo, not Paris. Perhaps even Hamlet, not Laertes. Besides, there are your designs. You want a place where you could have a permanent stage and play a few parts and bring some of those designs of yours to life. Or don't you? You'd have to work, you know — no time for fooling around talking about things. Oh yes, it could be in your precious Dublin if you like. Something like Peter Godfrey's Gate in London. And break away from Shakespeare for a bit. There are lots of exciting things from Russia and all over the place." [7]

But MacLiammóir had a special purpose in staying with McMaster for a little longer. He had at last completed the English script of *Diarmuid and Gráinne* for McMaster's company, with some help from Edwards in the construction of the last act. Edwards was already planning the production moves on the backs of envelopes or with chessmen, even with lumps of sugar. He told Micheál: "I'm going to talk to Mac about this play. Do you think he'd ever let me produce it? He's always saying he wants a producer, he's an actor all the time, production bores him really." [8] However, the last thing actors of McMaster's generation wanted was a producer. He regarded them as pestiferous busybodies — "a lot of silly little boys from Oxford or somewhere, don't know the stage from their elbow." [9] But there was his brother-in-law and, of course, Marjorie to consider so, with "absent-minded amiability", McMaster agreed to do the play in Kilkenny "in about a month's time". The billheads were printed and read:

The Theatre, Kilkenny
Anew McMaster in,
Diarmuid and Gráinne
A romantic play on an ancient Irish theme
by
Micheál MacLiammóir

It was all too good to be true: rehearsals never began. Marjorie had to break the bad news to her brother, saying that her husband had taken "one of his fits". McMaster explained it differently:

"We're all tired dear and we've just done *The Dream*. Yes. Oh yes. I like it very much, very charming indeed but it's not the time for it. No, perhaps we'll do it in the autumn. I can't face anything now. Can't face it. That's all it boils down to. Even Sarah [Bernhardt] couldn't face new plays all the while. I'm sorry to have to disappoint you, Micheál." [10]

McMaster was probably none too happy with his new Iago who threatened to filch from him his jewel of a juvenile lead. MacLiammóir for his part must have been disappointed by the Kilkenny billhead. Much as he wanted to see his work staged, he coveted star-billing in his own play. The plot thickened on a country road near Limerick where Coralie Carmichael, Edwards and MacLiammóir took shelter from the rain in a pub. "Now I've something to work for," the producer Hilton declared:

"We'll make a theatre if the only show we do in it is your bloody play. We three are going to get a bit of capital some-where, and we'll open in Dublin before the year is out." [11]

The days of the great actor-managers like McMaster were coming to a close. If he had played the lead in a Kilkenny production of *Diarmuid and Gráinne* the play would most likely have shared the fate of the unhappy collaboration of W. B. Yeats and George Moore on the same theme. Their *Diarmuid and Gráinne*, now deservedly forgotten except by academics, was staged at the Gaiety Theatre by the well-known actor-manager, Sir Frank Benson, in October 1901. This mixture of Wagnerian Opera and Celtic Twilight, with music by Elgar, was slammed by the critics; but a little play in Irish, *Casadh an tSúgáin* by Douglas Hyde, staged on the same night by a group of amateurs from the Gaelic League, was recognized as marking a turning-point in the development of Irish drama. For good or ill, a blend of folklore and peasant realism was about to supplant the grand manner.

Likewise, it was MacLiammóir's Irish language version of *Diarmuid agus Gráinne* that opened the way for a new develop-ment in Irish theatre. While Hilton Edwards was building theatres in the air, which would house not only MacLiammóir's play but the more daring experiments of Toller, Kaiser and

Ibsen, MacLiammóir was planning a production of his play in Irish with a Professor of Romance Languages at Galway University, Liam Ó Briain. Ó Briain, a Dubliner and veteran of the 1916 Rising, enthralled MacLiammóir when they first met in the spring of 1928:

One morning in Galway the landlady told me that Professor Liam Ó Briain wanted to see me. I went down and saw for the first time the small laughing eyes, shrewd and melancholy like the eyes of a countryman, yet full of a searching trustfulness; the beautiful white hair, the burly figure, and heard for the first time the cackling irresistible laughter of my best Galway friend. Our conversation was in Irish, and I had not spoken it for so long that when at that hour of the morning that never finds me at my brightest I listened to his news I wondered was it all a dream. For here, like a brilliant red herring across the nebulous splendour of Hilton's imaginings for a theatre of our own, was an offer that meant not only experience in production and management, but a practical opportunity for *Diarmuid and Gráinne* in its own language, and a chance to give to that language something at last that if its value were plastic only might be worth while. For I knew, whatever the faults of the play might be, that its settings alone offered a million occasions to producer and designer alike, and that a memorable barbarity on the stage of a Gaelic Theatre in the only Irish-speaking town we had left would create perhaps a model that might well have results on the future.[12]

When the McMaster tour ended MacLiammóir and Edwards returned to Galway to stage *Diarmuid agus Gráinne*. They auditioned university students, soldiers from the Irish-speaking battalion at Renmore Barracks, and scores of Galway people with an urge to act. Casting proved to be more Hobson's choice than trial and error. Among the final cast were Liam Ó Briain, who played Fionn MacCumhaill, and Máire Ní Scolaí who played Gráinne opposite to MacLiammóir's Diarmuid. A handsome girl and wonderful traditional singer but, with no experience as an actress, she must have made it difficult for MacLiammóir to achieve an exact balance and rhythm, especially in the love scenes. Also in the cast was Proinsias Mac Diarmada (Frank Dermody) then a soldier at Renmore Barracks who, after a training period at the Gate Theatre, became a producer in Galway and subsequently at the Abbey Theatre. Máirtín Ó Díreáin, then a Post Office clerk in Galway, played a small part.

A local committee had been formed to supervize the conversion of a disused hall in Middle Street, in the centre of Galway, into a small theatre; the reconstruction work took place during rehearsals. MacLiammóir planned the colour scheme for the building itself: the saffron walls, the red doors and woodwork; and the black and gold front-curtain with peacocks in a surround of Celtic design. He also designed the costumes and scenery for the production. Edwards, although nominally stage-manager, co-produced the play in a language which was foreign to him. He planned the lighting and, once rehearsals began, co-directed the cast with a mixture of confidence and incredulity that a playhouse and a play could be so quickly hammered into shape in a land noted for its dilatory approach to problems.

The country's first Irish-language theatre was christened *An Taidhbhearc* by Tomás Ó Máille, a professor at Galway University. Ernest Blythe, then Minister for Finance, had made the project possible by providing a small state subsidy — as he had done for the Abbey Theatre four years earlier. Blythe's advice to the founders was to experiment, to create something new, to provide "a machine" for the production of plays in an elegant fashion — and not to worry if the theatre was often half-empty in the first few years. After a glittering first night on 27 August 1928, attended by the Governor-General and several government ministers, Lady Gregory and various leading citizens the press proclaimed a new dawn for drama in Irish. *The Connacht Sentinel* wrote glowingly of the production and quoted Ernest Blythe: "It really strikes a new note in the matter of Irish plays. The setting and lighting effects were very beautiful." [13] Hilton Edwards was less certain, shrewdly observing that in a small country where amateurism abounds, initial enthusiasm is seldom sustained.

For MacLiammóir, the opening of the Taidhbhearc was but one highlight in what had been a remarkable year. He had written and staged what is still probably the best play in the Irish language, and he had played a major part in the establishment of the first theatre for the production of plays in the native tongue. After *Diarmuid agus Gráinne* finished its run MacLiammóir produced his own translation of *Prunella* by Granville Barker. But he did not stay long in Galway: before the year was out he and his partner had moved on to a new and exciting theatrical venture in Dublin.

In later years, the Taibhdhearc accomplished more as a training ground for new talent than as a theatre where playwriting flourished. Frank Dermody, a director of unharnessed genius; Walter Macken, a playwright, actor and novelist of stature, and the incomparable Siobhán McKenna perfected their crafts in the theatre in Middle Street. When MacLiammóir returned to Galway to redirect *Diarmuid agus Gráinne* on the twenty-fifth anniversary of its first production, he could not suppress a feeling of disillusionment. In a poem in *Bláth agus Taibhse*, he wrote of the new City of the Tribes:

Bean sciamhach i mbéal an bháis a bhí ionat:
Ach anois is mór m'eagla
Go bhfuil tú athraithe
Ag lucht do tharrthála
Go bhfuil tú athraithe cómh mór sin
Nach mbeidh ionat, go luath
Ach liopáiste pheacach,
Do ghuth mar phearóid
Do mheon mar theach cúntais
Do ghnúis mar pháipéar nuachta.

Once a beautiful woman in decline:
I greatly fear now

That you have changed
At the behest of your helpers
Changed so greatly
That soon you will be
But a gaudy slattern
With a parrot-like lingo
The mentality of a cash register
And the face of a newspaper.

Ten years later, when MacLiammóir returned to the Taibhdhearc for a performance of *The Importance of Being Oscar*, he was given a civic reception by the Mayor of Galway. According to a *Connacht Tribune* report he felt more optimistic about Galway, suggesting that it was a city that left an impression of what Ireland might have been if the English conquest had not taken place, because it was closest to the ancient traditions. MacLiammóir's fear was that Galway might accept what was worst in her search for what was called progress; he did not say that they go back to the old ways, but that they should preserve what was beautiful in the past. It was a heartbreak to see the Claddagh destroyed — and it would have been a great commercial attraction if preserved. Warsaw, for example, had been rebuilt from utter destruction as a medieval city. But at the end of all, MacLiammóir was always proud of his part in founding, in Galway, "the first Irish-speaking theatre in the world".

· V ·

The Starting Gate

"... where motley is worn."

W.B. Yeats *Easter 1916*

HILTON EDWARDS AND Micheál MacLiammóir decided in 1928 to establish in Ireland a new theatre for the production of international drama.

"Why Dublin?" asked Hilton. "Why not London? There are more people there."

"And more everything else," replied Micheál. "London has everything, Dublin next to nothing. What's growing must be fed."

"And so to Dublin we went," wrote Micheál in later years, "and part of me is sorry that this was so but the larger part is still glad."[1]

MacLiammóir knew that previous attempts to launch an art theatre for the production of world masterpieces had not been successful, and his earlier association with Edward Martyn's Irish Theatre in Hardwicke Street had proved to him that amateur enthusiasm, like patriotism, was not enough. A more ambitious venture than Edward Martyn's, The Dublin Drama League, had been launched ten years before by Yeats and Lennox Robinson for the production of plays not normally to be seen in the commercial theatres or at the Abbey. It was intended that some of these might become part of the Abbey repertoire provided that they did not interfere with the Abbey's main work of staging new plays by Irish dramatists. The Drama League plays were performed at the Abbey, which was rented to the League for a small fee on Sunday and Monday nights when there were no scheduled performances by the Abbey Company, many of the members of which took part in Drama League productions. Plays by Pirandello, Verhaeren, Strindberg, Toller and other European dramatists were well supported by the subscriber members; the only Irish-born authors represented were Shaw and Lord Dunsany. The policy of the play selection committee, elected by the members, was, as one critic put it, "not to court success but to produce brilliant failures". To that extent something of Edward Martyn's ideas survived for nearly a decade.

The Abbey, as had been envisaged, did extend its repertoire by occasional productions of plays such as *The Importance of*

Being Earnest, in 1926, and Eugene O'Neill's *The Emperor Jones*, in 1927. But Yeats and Lady Gregory remained firmly of the view that, even when there was a shortage of good new work, the Abbey should not change its policy of giving priority to the native drama. Yeats, in fact, opposed the regular production of foreign masterpieces by the Abbey Company on the grounds that such a policy would bankrupt the theatre. The contrary view was put forward in 1927 by Norman Reddin, a former actor with Edward Martyn's company, at a debate on "The Necessity of a National Theatre". He deplored "the endless cottage sets" to be seen on the Abbey stage and "the purple peasant who, when he was not cheating his brother out of a field or killing his Da, was whining and philosophizing into the mist that does be on the bog". Reddin, however, disingenuously ignored the emergence of O'Casey at the Abbey as a major playwright who offered a new and more critical view of Irish nationalism and politics.

Several splinter groups, eager to develop beyond the confines of Irish theatre, took their cue from the Drama League. The most notable, The New Players, staged the first Expressionist play seen in Dublin — George Kaiser's *From Morn to Midnight* — produced by Dubin barrister Denis Johnston in 1927. Earlier that year Johnston had accompanied O'Casey on a visit to Peter Godfrey's London Gate Theatre to see pioneer work in the Continental manner. It was mainly due to the work of the Drama League that there was a small and sophisticated audience in Dublin for an exciting new theatre, but few believed that two strolling players from McMaster's touring company would succeed where others had clearly failed.

Edwards and MacLiammóir were determined that they would build on the structures of the Drama League by adopting a more professional approach to the new wave in the theatre. They announced their ambitions in a night-club off Grafton Street where Madame Bannard Cogley, known as Toto to her friends, held her cabaret on Saturday nights. A lamp outside the door bore the legend "The Little Theatre" — an entity which existed only in the imagination of Toto and another habitue, Gearóid Ó Lochlainn, an Irish-speaking actor who had gained some experience of the Scandinavian theatre while working in the External Affairs office of the Irish Free State in Copenhagen. He too was an actor in search of an audience. He introduced Hilton Edwards to his actor acquaintances and to this somewhat sceptical group Edwards announced that he and his partner Micheál MacLiammóir would stage Ibsen's *Peer Gynt* on the fifteen-foot-square stage of the Peacock Theatre, the experimental annexe to the Abbey.

Most of the preliminary work for the staging of *Peer Gynt* in the one-hundred seat theatre was carried out by Hilton Edwards. A mailing list was prepared and subscribers were invited to become members of the Dublin Gate Theatre Studio. A circular announcing the first season of plays bore the emblem, designed by MacLiammóir in black and white, of a young thespian in a spotlight opening the gates of tragedy and comedy.

It is proposed to open the Dublin Gate Theatre Studio in October, 1928, for the production of modern and progressive plays, unfettered by theatrical convention. The London Gate Theatre has been extraordinarily successful, and the directors of the Dublin Gate Theatre are in a position to avail themselves of this organisation for procuring plays that would not otherwise be within the reach of Dublin Theatrical circles.

It is intended eventually to run the Dublin Gate Theatre Studio as a private theatre, and as soon as there are sufficient numbers, the Studio will be exclusively for these and their friends.

It is proposed to produce a play every fortnight. Produced upon a Sunday night, each play will run for twelve nights. There will be a performance each Sunday, but there will be no performance on Thursdays and no matinee.

It is hoped to hold from time to time lectures, discussions, and exhibitions of paintings for the benefit of members.

In addition to its Continental repertoire, the Dublin Gate Theatre Studio is prepared to consider, with a view to production, all plays of a suitable nature submitted. The Studio will utilize as much Dublin talent as possible. Engagements will be conducted upon a professional basis.

It is not the intention of the studio to encroach upon the activities of any existing Dublin theatrical organisation; rather it is the desire of the Gate to introduce a new element, both in the play and its production.

The directors were named as Hilton Edwards, Micheál MacLiammóir, Gearóid Ó Lochlainn and D. Bannard Cogley. While their manifesto was not the most resounding in theatre history, the list of plays under consideration for the first season would have strained the resources of Broadway and the West End combined: included were *The Adding Machine* by Elmer Rice; *Orphée* by Cocteau; *Gas and Kolportage* by Kaiser; *The Hairy Ape* and *All God's Chillun Got Wings* by O'Neill; *Brand*, *Peer Gynt* and *Hedda Gabler* by Ibsen; *Simoon* by Strindberg; *Six Stokers Who Own the Blooming Earth* by Elmer Greensfelder; *The God of Vengeance* by Sholem Asch; *Rampa* by Max Mohr; *Schweiger* by Franz Werfel; *Le Paquebot Tenacité* by Vildrac; *Theatre of the Soul* and *The Merry Death* by Evreinov; *Maya* by Simon Gantillon; *The Black Maskers* by Andreyev; *Diarmuid and Gráinne* by MacLiammóir; *Salomé* by Wilde; *Pelleas and Melisande* by Maeterlinck; and Goethe's *Faust*.

The list was ridiculously ambitious, but during their first two seasons at the Peacock Edwards and MacLiammóir succeeded in staging seven of the plays named, as well as eight others not listed. The selection of *Peer Gynt* for the opening performance was intended to mark the centenary of the birth of Ibsen and to give Hilton Edwards an opportunity to show his versatility as an actor in a most demanding part. MacLiammóir had taken the main honours at the Taibhdhearc; now Edwards as actor-producer gave Dublin its first sight of his artistry. MacLiammóir was not, however, entirely outshone as his settings did much to overcome the limitations of the Peacock stage, and the *Irish Statesman* critic C.P. Curran commented that "the freshness of the mountain farm, the dark encounters of the night, the grotesque horror of the trolls' hall within the hill — filled with the vileness of creeping things — were treated in stage scenes of great skill". MacLiammóir, still commuting between Galway and Dublin, did not appear in the second production, *The Hairy Ape*, but again designed the costumes and settings.

He reserved much of his energy for the third production which had, in a sense, been the *fons et origo* of the Dublin experiment — the staging of the première in English of his *Diarmuid and Gráinne*, in which he repeated his Galway success. Hilton played Fionn MacCumhail and Coralie Carmichael was Gráinne. Lady Gregory recorded in her journal:

> I . . . went to the Gate Theatre performance at the Peacock. It was *Diarmuid and Grania* (*sic*) by Micheál MacLiammóir — beautifully staged and lighted: no plot, just the simple story of Fionn and the Lovers. Simple language, a straight story very moving. It had been given in Irish in Galway and had been very successful there. A new departure. I felt far more in sympathy with it than with *The Big House* at the Abbey, going on next door.[2]

This was high and generous praise from a playwright who some thirty years earlier had written a play called "Grania" which was never staged.

Many of Dublin's literary celebrities who did not know Irish saw the production in English in the Peacock. C.P. Curran gave it a very favourable notice in the *Irish Statesman* but many, including MacLiammóir himself, were less than enthusiastic. Years later, disillusioned with "the noble lady, Romanticism", he wrote, "Once I fell in love with her and wrote a play *Diarmuid agus Gráinne*, a play I now dislike, and ever since I came to tire of it". The English text remained unpublished as the author found in it too many echoes of Wilde and Maeterlinck and only the Irish version, last staged by the Abbey Company in 1978, survived.

For its fourth production the Dublin Gate Theatre Studio staged the first public performance in Britain or Ireland of

Wilde's *Salomé*. Coralie Carmichael played the name part; MacLiammóir was Jokanaan, with Hilton Edwards as King Herod. Lack of money prevented the engagement of professionals in small parts. Some of the cast were scantily dressed because of the cost of hiring proper costumes, and actresses in small or walk-on parts were expected to provide costumes at their own expense. Delivered in a strong Dublin accent, the first soldier's lines — "The Tetrach has a sombre look" — raised guffaws. In the *Irish Statesman* Con Curran tactfully alluded to "a murmuration of untrained local accent".

Fund-raising events were arranged to supplement the small box-office returns. Lectures on various aspects of Continental theatre were given by A.J. Leventhal and Dorothy McArdle, herself a playwright and later the historian of Irish republicanism. A Gate Theatre Dance was organized by a fund-raising committee headed by Mrs Norman Reddin; the ever-faithful Aunt Craven gave a loan of fifteen pounds to balance the budget. MacLiammóir and Edwards spent Christmas with her in Howth in 1928, and could look back on a remarkable year in which they had established not one but two theatres. In *All for Hecuba* MacLiammóir recorded that he and Edwards felt "very tired and very poor" after two seasons in a theatre where "there wasn't room to swing a cat". With an endearing vagueness he added:

> Not that I believe we had lost any money — we hadn't any money to lose which made things very simple in those days — but we certainly hadn't made any and we seemed to live on boiled eggs and tick, Dublin being generously equipped in these things.[3]

Shades of *la vie de bohème* or, as a Dublin wit put it, "starving not in a garret but in Jammet's" — a restaurant famous for its French cuisine where "the boys", as they were affectionately called, were frequently entertained.

During the Gate Theatre Studio's first two seasons at the Peacock the fifteen plays staged conformed in the main to the avowed policy, which was to present plays of unusual interest and to experiment in methods of staging, freed from the conventions of commercial theatre. And with the success of this new venture there was no longer a role for the Drama League, which suspended its activities. The extent to which the Studio was a haven for avant garde theatre was limited, especially by international standards. Only in Dublin, for example, were John Galsworthy's *The Little Man* or *Juggernaut* by David Sears regarded as unusual. But to a considerable extent it provided a haven from the judgments of the Abbey. *Juggernaut*, which dealt in a naturalistic manner with an incident in the War of Independence, had won a Tailteann Games Drama Award but was rejected by the Abbey. In the same year the Abbey also turned down O'Casey's *The Silver Tassie*. Indeed, to be rejected by the Abbey became almost as much a recipe for success for a playwright as to be banned by the Censorship Board was for authors of books.

With a marked lack of tact Hilton Edwards wrote to O'Casey in England asking him to give the Gate *The Silver Tassie*, saying that while they "thought the play a bad one, it would do good business on account of the row raging because of the Abbey's rejection of the play". In *Sunset and Evening Star*, O'Casey hit back:

Oh very nice, nice oh yes indeed yes very nice indeed. Kill two birds with the one stone — do good business and hurt the Abbey. Though indeed the royalties, even from the Gate, would have been something of a Godsend at the time, the request was refused. Sean writing back to say that he was surprised that the Gate should wish to produce a play they were sure was a bad one.[4]

Though unable to cash in on the Abbey's rejection of *The Silver Tassie*, the Gate benefited when the Abbey failed to take on a play submitted under the title of "Shadow Dance" and under the playwright's name of E.W. Tocher. The author was in fact Denis Johnston, who was well known as the producer of The New Players. The manuscript was returned to him with a pencilled note in an unidentified hand: "The Old Lady says

No!" The author — and all of Dublin's theatre circle, with the exception of Lennox Robinson — believed that the "old lady" in question was Lady Gregory. In fact it was the consensus decision of the directors of the Abbey that the play required a style of production which was outside the range of the company at the time. This was, no doubt, true, but it was an admission of defeat. To sweeten the pill of rejection, however, the Abbey gave a small subsidy for a production by the Gate. Thus the author acquired a better title for his play and MacLiammóir got his opportunity to play a part which was the embodiment of the romantic Ireland so close to his heart.

The first scene of *The Old Lady Says "No!"* takes place in the garden of the Priory, Rathfarnham — a setting reminiscent of a romantic melodrama of an earlier era — where Ireland's most popular revolutionary hero, Robert Emmet, is visiting his beloved Sarah Curran. They declaim lyrical and patriotic lines culled from the anthologies of the nineteenth century.

Speaker (Robert Emmet): When he who adores thee has left but a name, ah, say, wilt thou weep!

Sarah: I shall not weep. I shall not breathe his name. For my heart in his grave will be lying. I shall sing a lament for the sons of Usnach.

Speaker: But see she smiles, she smiles! Her rosy mouth dimples with hope and joy; her dewy eyes are full of pity!

Sarah: Ah Robert, Robert, come to me.

Speaker: I have written my name in letters of fire across the page of history. I have unfurled the green flag on the streets and cried aloud from high places to all the people of the Five Kingdoms: "Men of Eire, awake to the blest! Rise Arch of the Ocean and the Queen of the West!" I have dared all for Ireland and I will dare all again for Sarah Curran. Ah it is a glorious thing to dare.

Major Sirr and his redcoats arrive to arrest Emmet. He strikes an heroic stance but is grounded by a blow from a musket.

Sarah: A star is gone! There is a blank in heaven. The last great tribune of the world is dead.

Then the audience senses that something has gone very wrong — that the actor playing the part of Emmet has been accidently injured in the stage blow. There is some confusion as Major Sirr comes before the curtain to ask if there is a doctor in the house. A doctor goes on stage to attend to the actor. It is only when there is a change of lighting to suggest a new scene that the members of the audience realize that they have been taken in by a brilliant *coup-de-theâtre*.

The play within the play takes place in the mind of the actor playing Robert Emmet, who imagines himself footloose in the Dublin of the late twenties in search of his beloved Sarah. The injured Emmet awakes in a city of shadows, surrounded by figures of nightmare conjured up by his fevered imagination. In his "delirium of the brave" he is bewildered by the incongruity between the romantic dream of Ireland and the harsh work-a-day reality and disillusion of the twenties. Sarah Curran is transformed into an old hag who pesters passers-by to buy a bunch of violets plucked in her four green fields. The virago is none other than Cathleen Ni Houlihan, the embodiment of Ireland and the ideals of nationhood. As the phantasmagoria ends, Robert Emmet dreams that he is back again in the Priory garden awaiting his Sarah. He looks at the city lights twinkling beneath him:

Speaker: Strumpet city in the sunset
> Suckling the bastard brats of Scots, and Englishry
> and Huguenot
> Brave sons breaking from the womb, wild sons
> fleeing from their Mother.
> Wilful city of savage dreamers,
> So old, so sick with memories!
> Old Mother
> Some they say are damned,
> But you, I know, will walk the streets of Paradise
> Head high and unashamed.
> There now. Let my epitaph be written.

Scores of ballads, songs, novels and plays had been written about Robert Emmet. No historical figure since Bonnie Prince

Charlie had had such a mesmeric influence on the Celtic consciousness. But the young romantic hero and ill-starred lover never found as fine an interpreter as MacLiammóir. It was more than a performance; it was one of these rare occasions in the theatre where the part — the mask — had become the person. The triumph could not have been achieved without Edwards' masterly handling of a difficult Expressionist text. The wealth of allusion presupposed a considerable knowledge of Irish literature and history; indeed, in the words of the producer, the script "read like a railway guide and played like *Tristan and Isolde*".

This success at the Peacock did not go unnoticed in official circles, and Edwards and MacLiammóir were invited by the City Fathers to create a pageant to be staged at the Mansion House during Dublin's Civic Week in the autumn of 1929. MacLiammóir prepared a script which covered seven episodes in Dublin's history, from the Viking Invasion to the Insurrection of 1916. With music by Dr John Larchet and direction by Edwards, MacLiammóir had another opportunity to project his new, heroic image, not only as Emmet, Owen Roe O'Neill and Patrick Sarsfield but, most importantly, as Pádraig Pearse, the leader of the Rising. The title of this masque of Dublin was *The Ford of the Hurdles*, but some commentators dubbed it "Micheál MacLiammóir through the Ages"! He had aroused what Yeats called "the spite of this unmannerly town" by now donning the mantle of Pearse, the twentieth-century reincarnation of Emmet. But MacLiammóir had known Pearse and his writings since his boyhood; he had illustrated, for his own satisfaction, a copy of *An Mháthair agus Scéalta Eile* (The Mother and Other Stories) given to him by his mother after the 1916 Rising. He also became aware of a latent homosexuality in some of Pearse's writings, such as the poem "*A Mhic Bhig na gCleas*" which he later translated into English:

Little lad of the tricks
Full well I know
That you have been in mischief
Confess your fault truly.

I forgive you child
Of the soft red mouth;
I will not condemn anyone
For a sin not understood.

Raise your comely head
Till I kiss your mouth
If either of us is the better of that
I am the better of it.

There is fragrance in your kiss
That I have not found yet
In the kisses of women
Or in the honey of their bodies.

MacLiammóir clearly welcomed the opportunity to play the role of Pearse, and the Rising episode of *The Ford of the Hurdles* was also played separately as *Easter 1916*. Later he designed a striking set for Pearse's *The Singer* and played the part of MacDara, the poet who cries out for a blood sacrifice. This identification with the work and ideals of a man who was also the son of an English father made MacLiammóir part of that company "who sang to sweeten England's wrong".

While contributing to the Gate's productions MacLiammóir continued to produce and translate for the Taibhdhearc in Galway and later for *An Comhar Drámaíochta*, a group that received a small government subsidy for the production of Irish plays in Dublin. And before the end of the 1929 season he returned to the Abbey as guest artist in Lennox Robinson's *Ever the Twain*. Another Gate player, Meriel Moore, who had distinguished herself in *The Old Lady Says "No!"*, was also invited to play a prominent part. Robinson's satire on those who undertook lecture tours of the United States in search of dollars from "the blue-rinsed ladies tea-club circuit" was a moderate success. MacLiammóir was pleased to be able to renew old friendships at the Abbey and described the play as "Robinson at his best, light as a puff-ball and inevitable as a sunrise". But there were many who believed that the sun was setting on the

National Theatre, for it seemed that the Abbey could do nothing right and the Gate do nothing wrong.

It was at about this time that MacLiammóir first met W.B. Yeats, after a production of Paul Raynal's *The Unknown Warrior* at the Peacock which both Yeats and Lady Gregory had attended. The following day an invitation came from Lady Gregory inviting him to lunch at the Standard Hotel so that he could meet the poet. Delayed at rehearsal, MacLiammóir arived a little late, only to hear the great man intone: "You told Lady Gregory you had wanted to meet me for fourteen years, you are exactly fourteen minutes late". However, Yeats added more kindly, "You are a magnificent actor".[5]

MacLiammóir later wrote that he was shy, unintelligible, and suffering from a new kind of stage-fright in the presence of the poet he

> had dreamed of all my days, not alone the seer, the visionary, the father of a whole nation's reawakening, but a most formidable man as well, an acrobat whose range was limitless, who threw you neatly to the ground before you were well within reach, and who, as you lay shocked and stunned, stood over you and paid you dazzling compliments; and remembering certain plays of his, I thought, "It's more than the Noh drama you've learned from Japan".[6]

They spoke of the London of the Nineties, of Wilde and Dowson, of Aubrey Beardsley and Lionel Johnson, of Beerbohm Tree and Florence Farr. What MacLiammóir liked best was that he had come face to face with a great man who was frequently dismissed as a poseur, and he had found that he understood and sympathised with what was for Yeats a defence mechanism.

> Of course he could pose, of course he could be both rude and arrogant. He could indeed be anything he chose, and the ability to assume all these qualities at will is a bare necessity of life for him who would spend his time in Dublin, where passionate and almost quixotic worship of mediocrity is coupled with an instinctive mistrust of the first rate, a permanent sense of discomfort in its presence, and a malicious determination to drown it in a storm of envy and belittlement.[7]

Both MacLiammóir and Yeats delighted in adopting a pose, using it not so much to impress as to keep bores and begrudgers at bay. In Yeats's case, the pose was hieratic, as befitted the primacy of the Bard. MacLiammóir's usual pose was half-humorous, affecting at times a mock solemnity, while a malicious twinkle danced in his hazel-brown eyes.

With the success of *The Old Lady Says "No!"* MacLiammóir's days of monastic poverty were coming to an end. The tenuous, nominal links with Peter Godfrey's somewhat ramshackle Gate Theatre Studio were over, and on Christmas Eve 1929 the Dublin Gate Theatre Company Limited was registered. Two new directors were appointed: Gordon Campbell, later Lord Glenavy, and Norman Reddin, an enthusiastic supporter, like all his family, of the Gate and earlier theatre ventures. The business and legal acumen of the new directors inspired confidence, and sufficient subscribers of shares came forward to enable the Gate Theatre Company to take a lease on part of the splendid Rotunda Buildings. On the second floor of the building the old concert hall, a large ornate room, was chosen for conversion into a four-hundred seat theatre. The architect for the project, Michael Scott, who had acted with the Abbey and Gate Companies, was later to design many of Dublin's modern buildings, including the new Abbey Theatre.

MacLiammóir had had a presentiment that he and his partner would one day work in the Rotunda. About a year earlier he and Edwards had shared a room in Groome's Hotel, from where they could look across at the Rotunda and ponder what might be behind the portico with the square pillars and the three tall dusty windows overhead. Now they knew:

The ends of tattered paper chains hung limply from lofty outraged corners; cobwebs stretched a malignant obscurity on the walls. . . . An hour later we stood at the door, looking across the street at Groome's Hotel. Hilton turned back and pointed up at the porch. "We'll have the name up there in lights," he said. "Just the one word — Gate."[8]

Everything is straightforward to the artistic mind but business and bureaucracy seem to bungle things. Mr Higgingbotham, the Dublin Corporation official responsible for the fire and safety precautions of public buildings, had a list of "dos" and "don'ts" which made the conversion of the old hall a tricky problem. MacLiammóir was responsible for the interior decoration and the painting of the proscenium curtain, a golden gate on a black background. He ran into trouble when he painted the toilet doors black with the words "*Fir*" and "*Mná Uaisle*" in gold leaf. On the final inspection Mr Higgingbotham asked the meaning of the strange inscription. When told that they meant men and ladies he enquired of the foreman which was which? Ignorance of the native language, Mr Higgingbotham insisted, could have dire results unless the English translations were added. An exasperated MacLiammóir painted the English signs as instructed, and added the appropriate words in eight other languages including Chinese.

The polyglot inscriptions, a scent of patchouli and Jeyes fluid, and a small coffee counter painted red and black provided the first impressions of anyone entering the theatre. In the auditorium alterations did not clash too strongly with the fine Georgian ceiling. The black surround focused attention on a wide stage which had no space overhead for the flying of scenery. On the floor below the theatre was a *Palais de Danse*, a sleazy place popular for "hops". During the quieter scenes of a play the band below could be heard playing foxtrots, rhumbas and the Lambeth Walk.

On 17 February 1930 MacLiammóir and Edwards welcomed a distinguished audience to the opening of their own Gate Theatre. The first play staged was Goethe's *Faust* with MacLiammóir in the name part and Edwards as Mephistopheles. It was a bitterly cold night and the heating system failed. But the warmth of the reception and the goodwill and support of a faithful few kept the new theatre open until a wealthy patron, a modern Maecenas, gave a measure of security to the most exciting artistic venture of the thirties.

· VI ·

Theatre Business

I am not much good at committee meetings, though the accusation against me that I never open my mouth but spend my time drawing Chinese faces on the back of the Agenda are not completely true.

Micheál MacLiammóir *All for Hecuba*

MACLIAMMÓIR USUALLY TOLD anyone who tried to discuss money with him that he had no head for figures and that Hilton looked after that end of the business, but if he did, he did not do so very well. The cost of renovating the theatre premises had exceeded the budget. On top of that, attendances were below expectations and all the plays they produced in 1930 lost money, including an enormous production of *Back to Methusaleh*, which was staged on three successive nights in October. The Gate was creaking on its hinges for want of "money from the greasy till", and soon the Board of Directors was issuing warnings of impending financial ruin. At the first Annual General Meeting of shareholders, on 12 December 1930, it can hardly have come as a surprise to the doodling director, MacLiammóir, that they were £700 in debt. Unless the 1,200 one-pound shares offered for public subscription were taken up without delay, the theatre would be forced to close.

At the AGM a portly, rosy-cheeked figure stood up to announce that he would buy the lot. Neither MacLiammóir nor Edwards knew who the new benefactor was; Edwards turned to Lord Glenavy who whispered, "It's Lord Longford".

Edward Arthur Henry Pakenham, the young man who had rescued them from bankruptcy, was the sixth Earl of Longford. Born in London and educated at Oxford, he had married Christine Patty Trew, an intellectual girl with vague Irish connections, in 1925. After the presumed death of his father at Gallipoli he had inherited the substantial Longford estates. From the family seat, Pakenham Hall in County Westmeath, Longford espoused Irish nationalism and, like another Irish peer, the kilted Lord Ashbourne, he learned Irish and spoke it at *Feiseanna*. Deeply versed in classical and Irish literature, he and his wife were intent on becoming involved in the Irish theatre.

Lord Longford was made a director of the Gate on the retirement of Lord Glenavy in 1931 and was appointed chairman in the following year. He did not see himself as any mere figurehead: he attended not only every production but nearly every performance in the theatre, sitting in the front row of the stalls with Christine by his side. Later, gathered backstage in the dressing-room or at supper in frowsy late-night restaurants along O'Connell Street, he would go through every detail of the night's performance with Edwards and MacLiammóir. The "first fine careless rapture" of the Peacock years was over and now the serious business of managing a bigger theatre was the responsibility of Hilton Edwards and Lord Longford. The days of amateurism were slowly coming to an end; more and more of the supporting players expected to be paid even while they were learning their craft. MacLiammóir and Edwards were thorough professionals, though for Lord Longford theatre was a rich man's hobby.

MacLiammóir's account of "the Longford regime" as he called it, was witty, frivolous and plainly partisan:

Lord Longford was beginning to take an active interest in the casting of plays and Hilton, reared in a tradition inflexible as that of the Samurai of Japan, shared with me the belief that casting was the business of the producer, so friction began on the board. In the matter of plays we would be led and advised, in the casting we were as obstinate as mules. And the meetings became overcast and sometimes thunderous.

It was all very difficult to deal with, because we were not doing well. Edward took to counting the house from his seat in the stalls, and sometimes it only took him a few minutes. Then he and Christine would come round after the performance and we would all say, "They don't want Restoration comedy," or, "They don't want translations from the French," or, "They don't want new plays by Irish authors."[1]

Whatever they may have wanted, they got new plays by Irish authors; not only Abbey rejects, but also plays by Lord Longford and his wife Christine.

Christine's first play, a comedy about *Berenice and the Emperor*, went on. It was sly and witty and outrageous, and I still chuckle with pleasure when I think of it, but no one came. . . . Then Christine's lovely *Jiggins of Jigginstown* made everyone realize that here indeed was a playwright with a new vision of Anglo-Ireland, preposterous and irresistible, and we played it happily for a few weeks until the failure of the public to understand Edward's magnificent translation of the *Agamemnon* as well as Denis Johnston's *Bride for the Unicorn*, plunged us into gloom once more.

It was not a merely financial gloom. Edward had nobly stood over the losses of *Agamemnon*, and he was ready with a loan for the Johnston play, which with all its obscurity had a quality of such insight and beauty that it made one revere, not the irony and technical skill displayed in *The Old Lady* but the plunging ecstacy of the poet's mind more than anything he had done before or since.[2]

Denis Johnston's second play, *The Moon in the Yellow River*, had been a success at the Abbey. It was more realistic and conventional than his other work and for this reason more acceptable to Dublin and the Abbey. His new play, *Bride for the Unicorn* had sufficient potential interest to bring Yeats to the Gate for the first time, but it was not a happy occasion. Accompanied by Lennox Robinson, he sat gloomily through the first act. When he could take no more, he rose from his seat and in the hearing of part of the audience and some of players commanded imperiously: "Lead me out Robinson!" When Robinson obsequiously did as he was told Shelah Richards, the Gate actress, who was then married to Denis Johnston, castigated Robinson, calling him Yeats's acolyte. MacLiammóir unkindly described the tall and lugubrious Lennox Robinson as "looking as if he were descended from a long line of maiden aunts". Yeats appeared to have escaped censure until Mary Manning, the editor of *Motley*, the Gate Theatre magazine, tried to organize a formal protest at the poet's bad manners. Foolishly she wrote to Sean O'Casey to ask him to lend his name to an exposure of the poet's behaviour, but the Green Crow, deep in Devon, refused to scratch at old wounds.

The supposed rivalry between the Gate and the Abbey was artificially cultivated; it had certainly not been the reason for Yeats's walk-out. When a caustic wit described the difference between the two theatres as being between "Sodom and Begorrah", knowing heads nodded. A host of such jokes did the rounds in Dublin in the early thirties and many of them, although later attributed to Oliver St John Gogarty and Myles na gCopaleen, were coined by James Montgomery, the film censor. Monty, as he was called, described MacLiammóir's performance in *The Marriage of Saint Francis* as "The Saint Francis of a Sissy". The Gate, striving to be different and challenging the conventions of a conservative theatrical capital, attracted gossips like moths to a candle. A teacher at Blackrock College, Fr John Charles McQuaid, later a formidable Archbishop of Dublin, advised his secondary pupils that the Gate was brilliant — but dangerous. In *No Profit But the Name*, a book partly drawn from Christine Longford's unpublished memoirs, John Cowell rightly comments that "the presence of Edward and Christine around the place brought to [The Gate] an air of respectability, of which it stood in some need. MacLiammóir's colourful flamboyance aroused a suspicious curiosity in Dublin's uptight ultra-conservative circles".[3] Indeed, the survival of the Gate in the stifling, repressive atmosphere of the thirties was a minor miracle.

In October 1931 a sixteen-year-old genius in the making began his stage career at the Gate. Two months earlier this tall, lumbering youth from Wisconsin had disembarked in Galway from the American liner SS Baltic. The precocious young man was called Orson Welles and had come for a walking and painting tour of Ireland. With him he had brought a copy of *Field and Fair*, the English translation of Pádraic Ó Conaire's short stories, strikingly illustrated by MacLiammóir, and, just as Ó Conaire had done years earlier, he had bought a donkey and cart with which to tour Connemara. He introduced himself at the Taibhdhearc as an experienced American actor willing to learn Irish and to act there, if the theatre would pay his way for a few weeks' study of the language in the Aran Islands. The shrewd Professor Liam Ó Briain, wary of touring actors ready to learn Irish in a few weeks, told him that the impoverished

Taibhdhearc was not in the travelling scholarship business. After a few weeks in Connemara Welles sold his donkey and cart to pay his way to Inisheer, the most westerly of the Aran Islands, where he wrote little and painted less. He then set out for Dublin.

After attending a performance of *The Melians* by Lord Longford at the Gate, he went backstage to present his compliments to Hilton Edwards. Edwards called MacLiammóir in to vet the prodigy:

"I've just told Mr Edwards some of the things I've done, Mr MacL'móir," he said, "but I haven't told him everything; there wouldn't be time. I've acted with the Guild. I've written a couple of plays. I've toured the States as a sword-swallowing female impersonator. I've flared through Hollywood like a firecracker. I've lived in a little tomato-coloured house on the Great Wall of China for two dollars a week. I've wafted my way with a jackass through Connemara. I've eaten dates all over the burning desert and crooned Delaware squaws asleep with Serbian rhapsodies. But I haven't told you everything. No; there wouldn't be time." [4]

His curriculum vitae, MacLiammóir remarked, "was less ripely coloured but contained, roughly speaking, a similar information". Hilton Edwards professed that he did not believe a word of Welles' palaver but nevertheless he gave him a part in Jew Süss. MacLiammóir viewed Welles's superb self-confidence with critical detachment:

He knew that he was precisely what he himself would have chosen to be had God consulted him on the subject of his birth; he fully appeciated and approved what had been bestowed, and realized that he couldn't have done the job better himself, in fact he would not have changed a single item. [5]

According to J. J. Hayes, the Irish correspondent of the *New York Times*, the sixteen-year-old played the part of a forty-year-old duke in Jew Süss with "naturalness and ease. . . . which at once caught the packed house in his first appearance". In his next part, that of a Montana millionaire in a forgotten play, *The Dead Ride Fast*, the same critic cabled: "I have never seen on any stage a more true-to-life portrait than that of the wealthy self-made American millionaire. . . . Played by Orson Wells (*sic*) the young American actor, 'Richard Bentley' came to life in most convincing fashion." Welles got another rave notice in an undistinguished play, *The Archdupe*, by Percy Robinson. After playing a terrifying ghost in *Hamlet* (in which he doubled as Fortinbras) he rounded off his Gate Theatre apprenticeship in a romantic piece of spookery called *Death Takes a Holiday*. He had told Edwards and MacLiammóir that he would stay longer if they cast him in the lead of *Othello*, but they put him off with promises of important parts in *The Apple Cart* and *Coriolanus*, productions of which they then postponed interminably. Welles attributed this to Micheál's jealousy of Hilton's initial interest in furthering the career of a new star.

Over fifty years later, in a series of interviews in 1983 and 1984 with his biographer, Barbara Leaming, Welles gave a wildly speculative and subjective account of his stay at the Gate. He referred to Edwards and MacLiammóir as "the doyens of the theatre known fondly about Dublin as Sodom and Begorrah". The original joke had lost something in the telling. But to explain MacLiammóir's jealousy, he added: "Hilton was a born hetero . . . and our friendship was the friendship of two men, with no sexual overtones. I think that bothered Micheál, that put him out of it you see — the *worst* threat you can imagine".[6]

Welles did admit to Barbara Leaming that MacLiammóir was "a really great Hamlet". Indeed, MacLiammóir's Hamlet was the outstanding performance not just of Orson's time in Dublin but of that decade in the Irish theatre.

MacLiammóir had pondered deeply on his approach to *Hamlet*, the Everest of so many serious actors' careers. At first he found it difficult not to be influenced by McMaster's virtuoso performance in which the lines rang out like the tolling of a chime of bells. He searched for an interpretation more in tune with the deeper, even the darker side of his own inner nature:

It is perhaps this passion to escape from the known world that makes *Hamlet* still the most modern of the plays in this age when many seem to be searching more consciously than before for new experience, for extension, for an expression of what is but dimly guessed at in the unexplored regions of the self; when the arts themselves seem to have grown restless, plunging from one locked gateway to another in their attempt to reach the mysterious house whose lighted windows beckon through the night. It is so with Hamlet himself, who had peered so long at the darkness through the bars of his cell that he had seen or fancied he had seen those windows shining in the dark; and his intolerable attitude towards Ophelia can be explained as well by his view of her as a symbol of what binds him to the earth as by this or that sexual inhibition.[7]

MacLiammóir planned a more poetic, introverted interpretation than Dublin audiences had seen. The encounter with the ghost of his father, the evidence of the King's crime as shown by his behaviour during the play scene, his mother's horror at accusations of guilt do not spur this Hamlet to action. Despite circumstantial evidence he shrinks as long as he can from a violent deed, preferring self-immolation.

Hilton Edwards, as producer, advised MacLiammóir to stop theorizing about the part and to act it in accordance with his own insights. Micheál took the advice:

An actor with a literary theory in his head is the most ineffectual of God's creatures. . . . I'm going to act Hamlet, not write a phoney book about him. There have been enough of those already. Really he is an over-discussed young man and if anyone had wanted to save him they should have given him a hard day at the wash-tub. Thank God nobody did, or there wouldn't have been any play.[8]

MacLiammóir acted Hamlet with a conviction and sincerity that made a lasting impression on both seasoned playgoers and young people seeing the play for the first time. Joseph Holloway, who had seen most of the best Hamlets since Sir Henry Irving, was in sympathy with this more modern interpretation:

His diction on the whole was admirable and laden with music and gentle pathos, and in his description of Yorick, the King's jester, and the To Be or Not to Be soliloquy, it reached the height of its beauty. He spoke each of these two speeches as if the thoughts arose in his mind as he spoke them aloud.[9]

Gabriel Fallon, a former Abbey actor and an "old buttie" of O'Casey's, was a theatre critic whose reviews were highly respected. In the *Irish Monthly* of March 1932 he wrote:

Here was a Hamlet wrapped up in his own reflection, thinking aloud. Here was a Hamlet who made no attempt to impress his words upon others by a studied exaggeration of emphasis or manner. A Hamlet who did not *talk* at his hearers. There was much (very much) of the gentleman and the scholar in him; and perhaps a shade — just a shade — too little of the actor. A pensive air of sadness sat — and sat reluctantly — upon his brow, but no appearance of fixed and sullen gloom. Weakness and melancholy were there, but harshness was not. Inevitably the most amiable of misanthropes, this Hamlet walked and spoke gracefully within the play, nor did he at any time, as many of his fellows do, straddle the footlights to split the ear of groundlings. He was not, as some are, a walking neurosis, nor yet an actor wallowing in a great part.[10]

Con Curran, always a sympathetic critic of Gate productions, praised MacLiammóir in the *Irish Statesman* for returning to their living place speeches which had shrivelled under the spotlight into "perfect dead members". These great speeches grew naturally from their context. He drifted into soliloquy like one to whom reverie is habitual. The outstanding characteristic of his Hamlet was its youth — youth lonely and outraged — and the interest of the performance lay in noticing how this quality enriched the tragedy. We have had so many middle-aged, foolish Hamlets, barren irresolute things born out of *Goethe* by Coleridge. This was the tragedy of youth not of irresolution.[11]

The playwright David Sears, theatre critic of the *Irish Independent*, wrote:

I have never used the word genius in a theatre notice, but I have no hesitation in applying it to the Hamlet of Micheál MacLiammóir.[12]

Having achieved this level of success at home the Gate had begun now to attract interest from overseas. The British Council invited it to present a series of plays in Cairo, and offered a guarantee against loss, but Lord Longford insisted that the invitation should not be accepted on the grounds that the Gate's proper sphere of activity was Dublin. It may be that his concept of nationalism did not favour the policy of the British Council whose avowed concern was "the spread of British culture overseas". Edwards and MacLiammóir were sorely disappointed but they were learning quickly that he who pays the piper calls the tune.

Lord Longford's attitude changed somewhat when the Gate Company was invited to play a three-week season at the Westminster Theatre, London, in 1935. *The Old Lady Says "No!"* and Lord Longford's *Yahoo*, a play about Swift, were automatic choices. And London, the centre of world theatre, argued Lord Longford, should also have an opportunity of seeing MacLiammóir's *Hamlet*. Hilton Edwards demurred. He suggested that it was bringing coals to Newcastle to stage *Hamlet* in London so soon after John Gielgud's resounding success in the greatest part in English theatre. It was highly unlikely, he pointed out, that Gielgud would bring *The Playboy of the Western World* to Dublin. As usual, however, Lord Longford had the last word. He insisted that London should hear Shakespeare as spoken in Ireland; artistic questions were resolved with a wave of the cheque book.

To Lord Longford's delight, *Yahoo* was hailed by Harold Hobson of the *Observer* as the best piece of Expressionism he had seen in the theatre. James Agate in the *Sunday Times* found the play woefully short of humour, a quality in which Swift's work abounded, but there was general approval of Hilton Edwards' performance as Swift. Denis Johnston's *The Old Lady Says "No!"* was hailed as a *succès d'estime* with special praise for the acting and production.

On the first night of *Hamlet* in London a wave of terror swept over MacLiammóir, leaving him "exhausted and vacant". "I stumbled mechanically through the play," he admitted, "and throughout the run I did not give one performance of distinction." [13] The press reviews referred condescendingly to the "Irish Hamlet" and James Agate delivered the *coup de grâce* when he called it "the broth of a Hamlet". As Edwards had warned, MacLiammóir was beaten by what he later described as "the only effective weapon the English have against the Irish, that bantering, indulgent smile of a kindly doctor for a fractious child". MacLiammóir failed to overcome the inherent bias; in London he huddled in corners, avoided parties and press conferences, scudding through the streets of the city of his birth "like a Russian spy in the heart of Wilhelmstrasse". He felt, he said, "like a self-made alien". [14]

The success of *Yahoo* brought a temporary truce in the unequal contest between Longford and his leading players. When there was a renewed invitation from the British Council to visit Cairo, with the inducement of an additional subsidy from the Egyptian government, Edwards and MacLiammóir were eager to grasp the opportunity to spread their wings and perhaps pay back some of the money they owed Lord Longford. But again he was adamant that if he was to continue to lose money on the theatre, it would be lost in Dublin. Gate director Norman Reddin supported him. Denis Johnston did not take sides, but suggested that if Edwards and MacLiammóir felt so strongly about the tour they should go at their own financial risk. Lord Longford consented and finally it was agreed that they would be billed as the Dublin Gate Theatre Company, opening in Cairo at the Opera House in March 1936 and travelling later to the Alhambra in Alexandria. It sounded exotic and exciting and most of the company were glad to travel, though there were others who called it "The Flight into Egypt".

They had just arrived in Cairo when the credentials of the company were questioned by the director of the Opera House.

He had a clipping from a London Sunday newspaper announcing that the Dublin Gate Theatre would revisit the Westminster Theatre with a production of Eugene O'Neill's *Ah, Wilderness*. The confusion had been caused by Lord Longford who, unknown to Edwards and MacLiammóir, had recruited new actors to play the O'Neill comedy and billed the company as the Dublin Gate Theatre. By this time an exasperated MacLiammóir felt that their company was like "a troupe of trick-cyclists from Nijinovgorod". "The boys" had been outwitted by the wiles of their patron and benefactor.

For some years Christine Longford had tried to keep the peace between her husband and the fractious partners. She wrote:

Hilton Edwards is a producer who is never satisfied with the second best. He extracts the last drop of significance from a play and the last ounce of activity from the actors and conducts his cast like the conductor of a theatre orchestra. That is why the Gate is Dublin's theatre of the nineteen thirties. Now that the little theatres of the world have done their best and are dropping into bankruptcy and the commercial theatre has done its worst and is making a belated search for new plays, the Gate retains its balance and is going straight ahead.[15]

In her novel *Printed Cotton*, which gives a thinly disguised picture of the Gate, she describes MacLiammóir as seen through the eyes of a young girl from the country.

When Martin Maulever came on I thought he was the handsomest man I had ever seen, and I had a thrill which I believe was almost entirely aesthetic. . . . It was a Russian play, and the scenery was beautifully painted in bright colours. Florrie whispered to me that Martin designed all the sets. She said, "People say he's partly Russian but I know for a fact that he's partly Spanish, and partly Norman-Irish".[16]

Under the guise of fiction Christine succeeded in flattering Micheál, but her admiration for him and his partner was not enough to heal the rift in the company. Though the five years of

Longford's reign had been rewarding for the Gate Theatre, it was now clear that there would have to be a parting of the ways. After discussions and some rancour it was mutually agreed that a new company, billed as Longford Productions, would play in the Gate Theatre for six months of the year and for the remaining six months would tour throughout Ireland. The Edwards-MacLiammóir company would take up residence at the Gate while Longford was on tour. This meant that if there was to be any continuity of employment for the cast, the Edwards-MacLiammóir company, Dublin Gate Theatre Productions, would also have to tour for several months of the year.

In retrospect it is surprising that such contrasting pairs as Hilton and Micheál, Edward and Christine, remained together for as long as they did. Micheál constantly poked fun at Edward's cackling laughter and his resemblance to an overgrown, overfed schoolboy while Hilton fumed and spluttered at his cheque-book dominance. John Cowell records Christine's grievance that if a new alpaca suit was tailor-made for Micheál in a part, it was never returned to the theatre wardrobe. Micheál's motto was, if the suit fits, wear it. MacLiammóir and Edwards had introduced Lord Longford to the magic world of the theatre, where he now felt ready to be his own Prospero.

· VII ·

Masks and Faces

"Put off that mask of burning gold
With emerald eyes."

W.B. Yeats *The Player Queen*

IN DUBLIN IN the 1930s Micheál MacLiammóir, with his toupée and heavy make-up, was one of the sights of the city. Only Jack Doyle, the singing boxer known as "the gorgeous Gael", attracted as much attention. Everybody knew or pretended to know Micheál; as he paraded Grafton Street or O'Connell Street he was saluted in Irish and English by passers-by, though scarcely one in a hundred would go to see him act. His niece, Mary Rose McMaster, saw him like Shelley plain:

> One of my earliest memories of Micheál was in Howth where we lived (in between our almost endless tours). Micheál and Hilton were sitting in the garden of an elderly lady we all called Aunt Craven. I was about eight years old and Micheál was turning an umbrella or parasol around his shoulder when one of the spokes hooked into his toupée and off it came! I screamed "Look, Uncle Micheál's hair has come off." "I don't know what you mean," he said, and quickly planted it back on his head. It was the only time I ever saw him without it. His black hair-piece was simply part of him as was the make-up he wore, it all seemed perfectly natural to me.[1]

Professional actors have always lived somewhat unreal and uncertain lives within the world of the theatrical community, but in a country where adult homosexual practice was repressed socially and was an indictable offence by law, the actor who showed such proclivities lived in doubly insecure circumstances. MacLiammóir would naturally have favoured a more liberal regime, but he was middle-aged before the Gay Rights Movement came into being. And when a campaigner then asked him to participate in a march to Dáil Eireann to make representations, he responded wearily, "My dear fellow I'll have nothing to do with it. They will only get us a bad name."

Fortunately for Dublin's claim to be a fair city, MacLiammóir never had to face the ignominy of a public prosecution like his colleague Sir John Gielgud in London. MacLiammóir's flamboyant lifestyle aroused jealousy even among fellow gays in the theatre, and he knew that two theatrical colleagues had made reports to the police about his conduct, but no charge was ever preferred against him.

In his adopted home town Micheál's flamboyance was regarded for the most part with tolerance and even affection, but when he and Hilton Edwards went, in 1934, to the Todd Festival at Woodstock, Illinois, their behaviour caused some surprise. In this American campus summer season Hilton played his old part in *Czar Paul*, Orson Welles was Svengali in *Trilby* and Micheál starred as *Hamlet*. According to MacLiammóir's account it was all very successful and not too demanding. But although the Chicago newspapers expressed their admiration of his acting, he was startled by a headline in the *Tribune* which read: "Irish Star Mislays Suspenders", and by a report that "MacLiammóir dreams the truth; no wonder the Irish believe in fairies".

Welles's account of the festival was more scabrous:
Oh it was wild because those two fellows were at the absolute high pitch of their sexuality — They were away from home and they went through Woodstock like a withering flame — It was a very strange summer because Micheál you know, wore what were then shorts of a briefness unseen on the Riviera and up and down the main street of Woodstock went Micheál, with beaded eyelashes with the black running down the side of his face because he could never get it right, and his toupée slipping but still full of beauty.[2]

In some ways Orson Welles and Micheál MacLiammóir were the opposite sides of the same coin; they touched nothing that they did not adorn. If Micheál's conduct at times bordered on the promiscuous, Orson, in those Woodstock days, portrayed himself as the perfect macho young man, monotonously propositioned by both sexes. Like MacLiammóir, Welles gave ambiguous accounts of his childhood and ancestry, dining out for years on imaginative flights of supposed autobiography.

After the festival Micheál and Hilton were taken on a bizarre holiday to New Mexico by one of the more eccentric associates of the Gate theatre. One day in Dublin Michael had received from a woman he had never met before a cheque for one hundred pounds and an invitation to lunch at the Gresham as a token of her admiration of his performance as Oberon in *A Midsummer Night's Dream*. His sixty-year-old admirer had turned out to be a rich Irish-American named Vivian Butler-Burke and she had informed him that she had known him in a previous existence as a Persian or a Chaldean! One day in St Stephen's Green she had presented him with the somewhat unexpected news that he was actually a Navajo Indian and that he would go to America to visit his ancestors. What she could not have known was that a telegram from Orson Welles had arrived that morning inviting MacLiammóir and Edwards to join him for the Todd Festival. And now, festival over, here the three of them were in New Mexico, meeting some Navajo Indians who, she insisted, had loved her in a previous existence.

Astral voices had told Butler-Burke to come to Ireland and she lived in Dublin beside the canal in a small Regency house filled with idols, icons and anti-vivisection posters. She visited archaeological sites where she prayed to the ancient gods and goddesses that they would make the Irish people understand her. MacLiammóir, ever trusting in his own psychic powers, sometimes accompanied her, on the grounds that "only the simple can accompany the great in the eternal cavalcade". He described her part in the evolution of the Gate as "incongruous, maddening and quite inexplicable", though explanation clearly lay in the welcome provision by her of financial support. Edwards thought her a phoney and a bore, although he did produce her play, *Bride*, which had won a Tailteann Games Gold Medal.

MacLiammóir had long since turned his back on his family in London, for it represented a past reality which conflicted with his own assumed identity as an Irishman. But with the death in 1934 of both his father and his sister Christine he felt compelled to acknowledge, at least to himself, the emotional ties that had not been entirely severed. His father, Alfred Willmore Senior, died on 3 June 1934 when he and Hilton were in the United States and he probably did not learn of the death until his return to Dublin in the autumn. But earlier in the year he had visited his father in London for the first time in many years, conscious that he was dying. Having married again, his father had a new family and had been working as a salesman.

It is difficult to know what MacLiammóir's feelings were. His references in his writings to his father's passing were almost perfunctory, and he revealed that during his father's lifetime "he felt ill at ease with him as he had never been with Sophie". He referred to him as "a kindly but remote figure with his adoration of fine pompous phrases and his alternate passionate love for, and violent rage on behalf of all his children". But the function of his writing about his family was as much to hide the truth as to reveal it. Micheál wrote that he remembered his father every night and, while his expression of this remembrance carries some conviction it also includes the characteristic insertion of a fictional Irish element in his family background. He thought of his father

in prayer and in fond images of his generosity, his singing of old Irish songs learned from his own father, his presents of goldfish and goldfish ponds, and of subtly carved wooden ornaments for the fireplace, of little delicate stools and tables, his brilliant line drawings — for his colour blindness prevented any possibility of his being a painter — his plays and his comic poems; as well as the effortless, eloquent stories of Beppo the Brigand, which he told extempore . . . every night in the darkness of the bedroom they shared for so many years.[3]

His account of his sister Christine's death on 6 September 1934 was more dramatic:

It happened that . . . the hideous warnings of Aleister Crowley [who had told Christine to beware of monkeys] were fulfilled. Tina was on a holiday in South Africa when, in a grove of palm trees near Durban, a monkey dropped down onto her back and bit her shoulder in the very spot that the magician had indicated. The bite developed rapidly into meningitis, and of this she died in the year 1934, filled with a terror that Crowley was sitting at the foot of her bed, watching her. Of course there was no one there, but the devoted friend who was nursing her sent for a Catholic priest who calmed and reassured her. She died in peace, but the Catholic cemetery where she was buried had to be guarded at the gate by the police, who successfully prevented the magician's followers from removing her body from the grave for the purpose of magical experiment. She will rest in peace, free from all evil, for power like that of the Great Beast cannot triumph over the love of God, and in her heart she had been aware of this all through her strange life.[4]

The emphasis on Christine's Catholicism at the time of her death was in keeping with Micheál's public declarations as "an Irish Catholic". He wished to be accepted not only as a convert to nationalism but also to the majority religion of his adopted country. He sought to be at one with the multitude in the matter of religious affiliation, yet he also maintained an independence of mind, cherishing Yeats's ideal of Ireland as a cultural entity transcending political, religious and sectarian differences, when most of those around him had abandoned it as a mere dream.

In Dublin comparative tolerance towards Micheál Mac-Liammóir's alleged and real deviance co-existed in a characteristically Irish manner with social, cultural and political conservatism. However, there was always a certain rather unhealthy curiosity in Dublin about "the crowd at the Gate", and this was fuelled in 1936 by the case of the Ball murder. The company had left on their first Egyptian tour and some camp-followers, including a pathetic young man named Edward Ball, wanted to follow them about at their own expense. It was alleged that he demanded money for the trip from his supposedly wealthy mother; when she refused he killed her in her home at Booterstown and threw her mutilated body into the sea. He was tried, found guilty but insane, and was committed to the Criminal Lunatic Asylum in Dundrum. There was an abortive attempt to rescue him by some theatre friends who tried to get him out of the country on a yacht. He was released eventually and emigrated to Australia.

Nearly thirty years later, when MacLiammóir was playing Hitler in *The Roses are Real* at the Vaudeville Theatre, London, he was surprised by a backstage caller.

Who do you think turned up one night among the milling throng that drive me dotty nightly, only Edward Ball that chopped up his mother in 1936, when we were on our way to Egypt. What do you think of that? A fine upstanding red-headed man in his forties but some Irish women (about my age) who were present visibly paled at his name.[5]

MacLiammóir, of course, had nothing to do with Ball's insane act but he and Edwards tended to be blamed for the indiscretions of anybody connected with the Gate. And there were incidents which convinced even hardened theatregoers that there was no smoke without fire. One of the Gate's popular variety shows, *The Dublin Revue*, included a ballet, *La Chevre Indiscrète*, in which a possessed goat is exorcised by a priest. The exorcism fails and, choreographically of course, a black ram is seen tupping a white ewe. Some of the audience booed or walked out and the father of one of the actresses, Florence Lynch, was so incensed that he came backstage and ordered his daughter to quit. The *Daily Sketch* reported Hilton Edwards as saying: "If anyone will give me a rational objection and courteously put grounds for removing anything from our performance, I will remove it, but we are responsible for the safety of the public and I will not allow riotous behaviour". MacLiammóir went even further: "I am an Irish Catholic, and I think political and religious protests which take the form of bullying and terrorising against young women during a performance are a disgrace to any religion". On the third night the *Irish Independent* reported that before the performance MacLiammóir announced that they still felt "that the ballet is inoffensive but rather than submit Miss Muriel Kelly [the choreographer] and the other ladies to a scene such as had taken place the previous night, we have decided to alter the scene to which objection had been taken". The priest and the acolyte with bell, book and candle were replaced by the Lord Mayor reading the Riot Act.

Throughout the controversy the writer of the offending scenario, Denis Johnston, kept quiet. Over thirty years later he told his biographer Harold Ferrar: "It was intended by me as offensive; it was anti-clerical".

Throughout the 1930s MacLiammóir tried to maintain a link with the Abbey Theatre, and in 1936 he accepted an invitation to play Naoise opposite Jean Forbes Robertson (the original Peter Pan) in a revival of Yeats's *Deirdre*, which was directed by a new producer from England, Hugh Hunt. MacLiammóir co-starred with this well-known English actress although the Abbey had always set its face against the star system, in principle if not in practice. In general the only way to become an Abbey star was to leave that theatre, as Barry Fitzgerald, Arthur Shields and others proved in their own good time.

The Gate was not slow to grasp an opportunity to star former Abbey actors. They invited Sara Allgood to play Madame Ranevsky in *The Cherry Orchard*, Mrs Millament in *The Way of the World* and the name part of Zola's *Thérèse Raquin*, a role which drew on her unique style and emotional power. The Gate could also claim the credit for letting Dublin see one of the Abbey's greatest players act for the last time in a straight part. MacLiammóir summed-up suitably when he wrote:

> So, as it is impossible to describe acting of this calibre, I will point to the real tragedy of Cathleen Ni Houlihan in being unable to hold such children close to her forever. Sally should never have been allowed to stay away so long.[6]

Another well-known Abbey actress, Ria Mooney, joined the Gate for two seasons in 1934, bringing with her an adaptation of *Wuthering Heights* by Donald Stauffer and herself. MacLiammóir as Heathcliffe, the farouche, wild-eyed gipsy boy of the Yorkshire moors, showed the demonic side of his persona to great effect. Ria Mooney gave what MacLiammóir described as "a dark and radiant performance that was aglow with flame". For her part she found MacLiammóir "utterly satisfactory" as Heathcliffe, and in every other part she played with him.

Another actor who appreciated both MacLiammóir and Edwards at this time was James Mason, who was a fine Brutus in the Gate's 1935 production of *Julius Caesar*. Years later he wrote:

I drink to the health of Hilton and Micheál. . . . It could be said that I am a constant celebrant since these two were my masters and I carry with pride the wrinkles that were imprinted during that happy year when I was attempting to measure up to their standards.[7]

Abbey actors tended to be silent about the Gate and trod warily around it. A malicious glee twinkled in MacLiammóir's eye whenever he detected a trace of begrudgery:

"I am a heretic about the Abbey tradition. . . . If you study it carefully and do not close your eyes to what is going on in contemporary England, you will see that its acting tradition is as derivative as our own at the Gate, except in the matter of dialect. It was a reaction against the type of work made famous by people like Julia Neilson and Martin Harvey, against velvet and heroics and ostrich plumes, against the operatic manner of the West End *fin de siècle*, in fact, and there already Wilde has said of George Alexander, "he does not act, he behaves!" So these actors, with the glorious exception of Sara Allgood and Máire O'Neill and a few others, behaved, and their behaviour was Irish and not English, but neither was it acting. And behaviour upon non-Irish stages, long before the Literary Theatre of Dublin had begun to lure young writers to the creation of Irish drama, was nothing new. The real achievement of the Abbey was the invention of a new tradition in writing, not in acting, for what in acting did it invent that was not being practised elsewhere by seekers after reality? One thing: the use of authentic Anglo-Irish speech. No, the Abbey has produced at least two actors and three actresses of supreme talent but it has never been an actors' theatre: its original title of Literary Theatre showed where its heart lay, and it greatest artists, with the exception of McCormick, have left it for London or for Hollywood; and if ever the Abbey or our own Theatre produce a new tradition of acting it will be a child of the future: nothing has yet been seen apart from a natural accident of voice and speech to make us distinctive as the French actor, for example, is distinct from the German or the English from the Serbian." [8]

He referred to the Gate's aim to present an alternative to what he termed the "bacon and cabbage" of the Abbey and concluded, with a Yeatsian flourish, "A manner must grow out of the life of the nation". While the words were MacLiammóir's the voice was that of Edwards, the unrepentant Englishman who could never quite rid himself of an air of superiority and who viewed the Abbey as more a literary movement than a theatre:

> Ever since we started, the Abbey has been rammed down our throats, and we have been thrust at the Abbey. There was no attempt at rivalry between the two theatres and our technique, our repertoire, our style of acting, seems to preclude any comparison. [9]

The pressure of work at the Gate during the thirties and early forties meant that Hilton and Micheál had few opportunities to attend the Abbey. MacLiammóir was apologetic about his lack of first-hand knowledge of the work of the Abbey when he lectured there during the Abbey Theatre Festival in 1938:

> Of Lennox Robinson's later plays like *Church Street* I regret that I have nothing to say about them. That's what comes of being an actor, I can never see the Abbey plays when I want to, because I am always working at the Gate; and whenever I am playing some part I would particularly like my friends to see — and all of my friends who don't work in the Gate work in the Abbey — they can't come, for the same reason. For years now I have not seen Delany or Richards or Crowe or May Craig at work, or the latest developments of McCormick or Dolan, or Cusack or Arthur Shields, my oldest Dublin friend. This is to me a matter of deep regret, because

apart from sentimental reasons, I believe firmly that actors can learn much from each other, that our honest opinion of each other's work, is more constructive than any other criticism, and that, next to that mysterious thing the united audience, there is no purer critic of acting than the actor. The author gives us the raw material for our dish; the producer gives us the instructions for our cooking; we serve it up ourselves, and the critics praise or blame; but it is that dark and mysterious body of potential enemies or potential loves out there in the blackness of the auditorium that teaches us nightly where the sauce is too thick or the dressing too sharp, and it is our fellows who can help us with dashes of salt and sprinklings of pepper, and I have always felt that one of Lennox Robinson's unique qualities as an Irish dramatist is that, alone among his fellows in Dublin, with the possible exception of Denis Johnston, he understands the actor, has lived and worked with the actor, has acted himself, and knows our qualities and defects, our peculiarities and vanities and jealousies and illusions, and all our funny little ways.[10]

Notwithstanding the overheated culinary metaphor, MacLiammóir showed that he could be generous in praise of the achievements of his fellow actors.

Despite his special relationship with his partner, MacLiammóir did not quite approve of the growing dominance of the director in the theatre. Edwards was one of the first of a new breed of directors who exerted complete control over every aspect of a production — lighting, costume, decor and the performance of the cast. Whether the play was ancient or modern, his aim was to give it the proper style of theatrical expression. The actors marched to his orders as if he were a general marshalling his troops. As Christine Longford said, he orchestrated his productions, treating the text as a musical score. He was an innovator and had often to work with performers who could not read a score, never mind play it. The less accomplished players were manipulated and cajoled into giving performances greater than their individual competence, while the accomplished soloist was often unnerved. Cyril Cusack, who played for a few seasons with the Gate company, did not respond well to Edwards' rather hectoring approach. Rehearsals were often stormy affairs and, on one occasion, the young and agile Cyril threw a few punches at Edwards, though without landing a blow.

MacLiammóir, unlike Cusack, did not rebel against the new tyranny; he just sulked at rehearsals after having been subjected to abuse. Mary Rose McMaster

admired Hilton as a director but was intimidated by him and I didn't like the way he humiliated Micheál in front of the cast. I was always on Micheál's side but as I grew older I could see that Micheál could be quite irritating sometimes. I was vaguely fond of Hilton as one is of an unattractive bull-dog who has always been around since you can remember but there were times when I really disliked him.[11]

Mary Rose may not have seen that Edwards criticized his leading actor publicly in order to intimidate the supporting players and make them realize that they might be next to feel the lash of his invective. But she was well aware that sometimes the rehearsal ructions continued in private:

I went often to Micheál and Hilton's flat in Dawson Street [over Maguire and Gatchell's Hardware Store]. Hilton, it seemed to me then, was always in a rage and he would throw books and papers, candlesticks, etc. in all directions; one day he threw all the silver and plates off the dining-room table! Micheál rarely answered back but would sit there silently looking like a martyr with his eyes toward heaven! At the time I felt sorry for Micheál but realized that he did sometimes provoke Hilton and that this was part of their relationship. When things became too "hot" we'd leave and walk around Stephen's Green for what seemed like hours; Micheál would tell me lovely stories from Irish folklore and try to teach me Irish. One day he bought me a silver watch at Louis Wine's in Grafton Street and had my name and his and Hilton's engraved on the back. He could be generous but also tight and knew it. He said he'd never learned how to spend money, having had so little in his youth.[12]

The tours to Egypt, Greece, Malta and the Balkans in the years before the Second World War reduced the tensions caused by the pair's clash of temperament. At times, though, they fought like cat and dog, or, indeed, like man and wife. Whenever Hilton Edwards mentioned these lovers' quarrels he quickly added that he and Micheál never let the sun go down on their anger. As dress rehearsals in those years often lasted all night, the sun must have come up sometimes before peace was restored. Yet in their life together Hilton brought a steadfastness and purpose to the wavering artistic ambitions of his partner. Edwards, with a mother named Murphy, possibly had more Irish blood than the self-styled Micheál MacLiammóir. Nobody in Ireland, of course, believed this. Edwards, like most people who got things done properly in the topsy-turvy world of the theatre, made enemies, but the uncompromising Englishman had the advantage that he could get the Irish to work much harder than they would for one of their own.

At times he disapproved of Micheál's offstage histrionics in St Stephen's Green or Grafton Street, for in all of his fifty-five years in Dublin Hilton was never tempted to act the Irish-man; he preferred to be the Svengali who could cajole Micheál to play that part to perfection. While Micheál was immensely proud of his Irish passport, signed personally by Eamon de Valera at the commencement of the Second World War, Hilton never bothered about naturalization papers, nor did he seem emotionally involved with anything more Irish than Micheál MacLiammóir. Although younger than MacLiammóir, Edwards always looked older. "Nobody cared," he once said, "what a producer looked like". In one sense, that male friendship was Platonic in the original Greek meaning of the term.

On social occasions Hilton would often play a supporting role so that Micheál could be the star attraction. MacLiammóir would enter like a Renaissance courtier who, with a turn of the head or the flash of an eye, could time a witticism like a rapier thrust. With the disarming insincerity of the born charmer, he was the darling of the drawing-rooms of Merrion Square. Hilton lacked the *plámás* to avoid the acrimony and malice which often passed for conversation in Dublin. At some of their own splendid parties Hilton fed Micheál with opportunities for *bon mots* until the conversation flowed without inhibition. Such was Hilton's devotion to and admiration of Micheál that he loved to see his partner and protégé dominate in any company.

As partners in the theatre Edwards and MacLiammóir were often fallible in their choice of new work, though they became more careful over the years. After the split with Longford there were fewer productions of new plays at home. They presented an Abbey reject, *The Demon Lover* by Lennox Robinson, which failed to impress the critics or the audience. In a fine production of Ibsen's *Brand* in 1936 MacLiammóir was excellent but the play was nevertheless a box-office flop. Eugene O'Neill's *Mourning Becomes Electra* and Auden and Isherwood's *The Ascent of F6* did not get the support they deserved. A fortunate choice was Emlyn Williams's thriller *Night Must Fall* in which MacLiammóir, as Danny, gave a performance that was more fully rounded than that of Robert Montgomery in the film version. MacLiammóir occasionally made a hit in cameo roles like that of the Mayoman up for the match in the tenement play *Marrowbone Lane* by Robert Collis, a doctor who used the theatre to shock middle-class audiences into an awareness of social evils in the Dublin slums.

The declaration of war by Great Britain on Germany had mixed consequences for the Gate. Of most immediate financial concern was the fact that British Council tours would no longer supplement the unpredictable box-office take at home. A particular problem was also presented by the wartime censorship which was employed by the government as part of its policy of neutrality. Lennox Robinson, in his adaptation of Maupassant's *Boule de Suif*, which he titled *Roly-Poly*, had transposed the action from the Franco-Prussian War to the invasion of France by Germany in 1940. The fact that in the play the French prostitute, named Roly-Poly, refused her favours to the German officer was taken by some in the charged atmosphere of the time to mean that the play had departed from the required standard of neutrality. Neither the French nor the German Ministers who attended were amused; both made representations to the Department of External Affairs and the play was officially withdrawn on the third night, although it was performed "privately" to an audience who were refunded the cost of admission.

The incident opened old sores when Lord Longford wrote to the *Irish Press* disassociating himself and his company from any responsibility for the production. How he could have been held responsible was puzzling, as he was on tour in the provinces at the time. Edwards and MacLiammóir rubbed salt in the wounds by publishing a sharp reply:

We are happy that the combined work of Guy de Maupassant and Lennox Robinson should have had, among other excellencies, the result of this bringing to light a statement too long left unmade by any but ourselves. We started our work in 1928, before we had ever heard of Lord Longford in connection with the world of theatre, and our mutual association during six years has already taken its place in past history.[13]

The war, although it closed doors into Britain and Europe, opened a new door at home. The Gaiety Theatre depended greatly on cross-channel shows for most of the year, except for Christmas pantomime and a few home-produced musical and operatic performances. While the war continued visits from touring companies were practically impossible and the commercial theatres had to depend on local talent if they were not to go dark. The managing director of the Gaiety, Louis Elliman, who also controlled the vast Theatre Royal, invited Edwards and MacLiammóir to play regular seasons in the plush-and-gilt Victorian theatre in South King Street. For MacLiammóir the Gaiety had a whiff of His Majesty's Theatre, and in the wings were shadows of the idols of his youth who had performed there — Bernhardt, Pavlova and Beerbohm Tree.

er a Goldfish, first stage appearance, 1911

Alfred Willmore by Robert Clarke, 1915

he Damsel I Left Behind Me, Punch 1915

Micheál MacLiammóir at Howth Head, 1920

Madonna of the Roads: A Memory of Máire O'Keefe

Cuchulain Fighting the Waves, 1926

Set for *Peer Gynt*, 1928

Designs for *The Old Lady Says "No!"*, 1929

MacLiammóir as Robert Emmet,
The Old Lady Says "No!", 1929

MacLiammóir as Sidney Carton, *A Tale of Two Cities*, 1945

Micheál MacLiammóir, Orson Welles, Hilton Edwards and Maura Laverty, 1949

Padraic Colum, Lady Longford and Micheál MacLiammóir in Jammet's

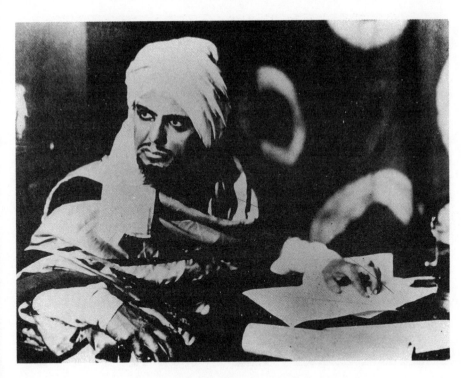

MacLiammóir as Othello, *Othello*, 1945

Orson Welles as Othello, MacLiammóir as Iago, *Othello*, 1949

MacLiammóir as Hamlet, Eithne Dunne as Ophelia, *Hamlet*, Elsinore 1952

MacLiammóir as Aleel, *The Countess Cathleen*, 1953

MacLiammóir as Gypo, *The Informer*, 1955

Bust of MacLiammóir by Marshall Hutson, 1952

MacLiammóir playing some favourite music at 4 Harcourt Terrace, 1953

The Importance of Being Oscar, 1960

The Importance of Being Oscar, 1960

Jacob's Television Awards, 1964; Charles J. Haughey, Micheál MacLiammóir, J.B. Jenkins

Michael Scott, Hilton Edwards, President Ó Dálaigh, Micheál MacLiammóir, Siobhán McKenna, Micheál Ó hAodha, *Áras an Úachtaráin* 1975

Hilton Edwards and Micheál MacLiammóir outside the Gate Theatre

Micheál MacLiammóir, 1977

· VIII ·

Hadn't We the Gaiety?

The modern theatre has died away to what it is because the writers have thought of their audiences instead of their subjects.

W.B. Yeats *Plays and Controversies*

THE "GATE AT THE GAIETY" season began in February 1940 with a theatrical *tour de force*, the première of MacLiammóir's new play *Where Stars Walk* in the presence of the President, Douglas Hyde. The curtain rose on a dimly-lit stage with a glissando of harp strings and a voice chanting of the Land of Faery

Where nobody gets old and godly and grave,
Where nobody gets old and crafty and wise,
Where nobody gets old and bitter of tongue.

When the lights went up to reveal the modern drawing-room of a retired middle-aged actress who had brought a group of friends along to rehearse a verse play written by one of them, there was an audible sigh of relief from an audience tired of re-enactments of an ancient age. Instead, the Land of Heart's Desire had intruded on the sophisticated tittle-tattle of Merrion Square in the person of the houseboy, Martin (Mac-Liammóir) and the maidservant, Eileen (Meriel Moore), who were the reincarnations of the god and goddess Midhir and Etain. Brittle and delightfully malicious gossip was blended with fantasy as the houseboy and the maid became concious of their ancient destiny; at the final curtain they took flight from modernity in the shape of two swans. If J.M. Barrie's *Mary Rose* had been rewritten by Noel Coward the result would not have been more surprising. This neo-romantic make-believe was wildly applauded. In his curtain speech the author addressed the President in Irish; later he recalled the sight of Douglas Hyde in his box "beaming with pleasure; at eighty-odd years the youngest man in Ireland".

The Gaiety, with over a thousand seats, made new demands on the partnership who were now attempting to reach the targets set by the manager Louis Elliman. There was a greater concern than before to present the best of the past with a sharp eye on the box-office. Nevertheless, there were some notable Shakespearean productions: *Hamlet* in modern dress, which for MacLiammóir meant a dress-suit, and soon afterwards a finely-judged performance of *Antony and Cleopatra*. Edwards got his chance to show that his acting had not been impaired by his directorial responsibilities in revivals of *Peer Gynt* and *Czar Paul*. A guest appearance by Dame Sybil Thorndike in Ibsens's *Ghosts*, in which she played Mrs Alving, spurred Mac-Liammóir to new heights as Oswald. With rare exceptions leading parts were shared between MacLiammóir and Edwards, and if there were any arguments about who should play what they were usually resolved by not doing the play at all. This happened in the case of John Coulter's adaptation of *Oblomov*, which was announced for production but never reached the rehearsal stage. Coulter was convinced that both MacLiammóir and Edwards had ambitions to play the title part. The partners continued to argue about who should play it until Spike Milligan, with his special kind of Goonery, prepared a stage version, jumped into bed as Oblomov and so settled the argument, much to Coulter's annoyance.

Few potential usurpers were allowed into MacLiammóir and Edwards' domain: if at times there was war it was a war of the roses, not a war of succession. One of the few exceptions was when they extended an invitation to McMaster to play his finest part, Othello, at the Gate and on the second Egyptian tour in 1937. He also appeared with the company at the Gaiety in 1942 when he played the part of an old-time Shakespearean actor in *The Light of the Heart* by Emlyn Williams.

During the first season at the Gaiety there were signs of a change of policy at the theatre. Popular cinema successes, or "plays of the film" as they were called, were staged in an effort to attract new audiences. *The Masque of Kings* was the stage version of the cinema hit *Mayerling* starring Charles Boyer. Daphné du Maurier's *Rebecca*, Walter Greenwood's *Love on the Dole* and Patrick Hamilton's thriller *Gaslight* came soon after the successful movies. Broadway box-office hits like *Arsenic and Old Lace*, *Uncle Harry* and *The Man Who Came to Dinner* were the kind of plays which packed the Gaiety for weeks on end.

In his booklet *Theatre in Ireland* MacLiammóir wrote a little sadly of the growing taste for the West End and Broadway commercial success, never in the English language to be done quite as well by Irish actors as the British or American ones, so that in the moment of their performance or in the enjoyment of their results there is always the dull concience stricken pang, that one is doing or reaping the benefit of a slightly second rate thing; a thing which one knows can be and has been done more perfectly elsewhere.[1]

The Gate, to the surprise of many of its admirers, never nurtured a major playwright as the Abbey had in the cases of Synge and O'Casey. Indeed, it failed, almost from the beginning, to attract a steady succession of playwrights who could have given it a distinctive and individual voice. In the forties and fifties it became more a showcase for the classics and international successes than a creative stimulus for new writers. Again MacLiammóir sounded a note of disillusion:

So there was lots of love and belief in our work and a good deal of squabbling and disappointment as well; a feeling among us at the Gate that having brought much of the world to Ireland we had but little of Ireland to show to the world when we went away, — a few fine works by Denis Johnston, a play or two of my own, some players fitted for their craft, and above all I believe some discoveries in production by Hilton Edwards that have made all seem worthwhile.[2]

From time to time there were productions of new plays by Denis Johnston, David Sears, Robert Collis, Frank Carney, M.J. Farrell (Molly Keane), Donagh MacDonagh and Maura Laverty, but only Laverty gave the Gaiety what it needed most — a box-office hit. She wrote entertaining, naturalistic plays of Dublin working-class life: two of these, *Liffey Lane* and *Tolka Row*, were later to form the basis for the first successful home-produced television serial. She also gave MacLiammóir an opportunity to play a character role for the first time, though whether he really welcomed this opportunity to submerge his carefully-cultivated persona in the part of an old codger is doubtful to say the least.

The one playwright who might have set his seal on this aspect of the Gate Company's work was Denis Johnston. The Gate had staged *The Old Lady Says "No!"*, providing Mac-Liammóir with one of his best-loved roles, and although *Bride for the Unicorn* had not been a success, Johnston was the best situated and most suitable candidate for the role of Gate playwright. But his only contribution to the repertoire of the Gate at the Gaiety was *The Dreaming Dust*, a skilful exposition of his theories about the Dean of Saint Patrick's which he expounded later in his book, *In Search of Swift*. Instead, most of his later work was staged at the Abbey (with the exception of *The Golden Cuckoo*, first produced by Long-ford Productions).

Johnston was an exceptionally talented man of considerable intellect who spread his wings in radio and television and as a brilliant war correspondent for the BBC. His acknowledged indebtedness, especially in his early years, to MacLiammóir and Edwards is unquestionable. But in *Sunset and Evening Star* Sean O'Casey wrote of a visit by Johnston to see him in Devon and of how Johnston

> seemed to be tired of the Gate; for he talked of it in a tired way, as if it were to him but the acrid dust of fireworks that had gone up the night before to make a dark sky falsely gorgeous, to spray the dark sky with fictitious gauds. Each production was as it were a trooping of the colours. They tired me in and they tired me out. Most things were done in a tiring, caparisoned rush. MacLiammnóir (*sic*) was getting tiresome, too, in that he still wanted to do the parts of young and handsome laddies though years had rubbed his bloom away, and a fattening chin had hidden the dear reflection of redolent youth that had stood before the back curtain of age when life was younger. Ah, me, we all diminish when the musk departs from the rose.[3]

MacLiammóir showed no immediate rancour in response to O'Casey's barbs, but in a diary entry for 2 June 1949 he noted:

> Have read nothing since I came here [Rome] except O'Casey's Innis Fail, Fare Thee Well (*sic*) which fills me with admiration

and deep, deep dislike. It made me wish more than ever that Ireland showed signs of a new mood in letters, as the nail-biting, tooth-baring school, still fashionable among writers whether they remained in Dublin or take refuge in Devonshire, become wearing to the nerves in the end, however dazzling in execution; there is much to be said for the creation of a new era of generosity.[4]

MacLiammóir perhaps realized the truth of the comment that he still wanted "to play the parts of young and handsome laddies", as O'Casey put it. He had lived so long enclosed within the crystal bowl that the actor-playwright in him was isolated, protected from the rough and tumble of life outside.

If Denis Johnston put his trust in the Abbey and in Longford Productions rather than the Gate, there was nothing much MacLiammóir could do about it except write more plays of his own. After *Where Stars Walk* he wrote seven more full-length plays especially for the Gate Company: *Dancing Shadow* (1941); *Ill Met by Moonlight* and *Portrait of Miriam* (1946); *The Mountains Look Different* (1948); *Home for Christmas* (1950); *Slipper for the Moon* (1958), and *Prelude in Kazbek Street* (1973). He also wrote a short play in Irish, *An Bréagaire*, which was produced at the Abbey and later translated as *The Liar* and produced at the Gate in 1969. In addition his adaptations of *The Picture of Dorian Gray*, *A Tale of Two Cities*, *Doctor Knock*, *Jane Eyre* and Liam O'Flaherty's *The Informer* revealed his sure craftsmanship.

The *Informer* gave MacLiammóir an opportunity to play the part of the spy, Gypo, in which role Victor McLaglen starred in John Ford's Hollywood film. Like his performances as Old Dan in *Liffey Lane* and *Tolka Row*, this transformation of the middle-aged actor who played juvenile leads amazed those critics who had complained that MacLiammóir was always the same. But unlike Doctor Johnston's dog, the wonder was not that it was done competently but that it was done at all. The part that he had written for himself in *The Informer*, that of the swashbuckling IRA man, was actually played by a youthful Denis Brennan. On the other hand, most of his own adaptations gave him parts that he really wanted to play. His Lord Goring in *The Picture of Dorian Gray* was like a five-finger exercise for the virtuoso performance which came later in *The Importance of Being Oscar*.

The best of this respectable output by a journeyman playwright had been written with roles specially suited to the talents of leading members of the Gate Company. He wrote tailor-made parts for himself in most of the plays and for Hilton Edwards as Prosper in *Ill Met by Moonlight*, and other roles were typecast for supporting players like Christopher Casson, Liam Gaffney and Robert Hennessy. Parts were specially written for Meriel Moore, Coralie Carmichael, Eithne Dunne, Peggy Cummins, and MacLiammóir's neice Sally Travers. Christine's daughter, Sally, had joined the company just before the war; a vivacious, good-natured person, she was, apart from Marjorie McMaster, the last and closest link with his family in London.

Many of MacLiammóir's plays were written to suit an immediate demand; they were works of their time providing rewarding parts for the actors and actresses who were available during and immediately after the war. They are infrequently produced nowadays and when staged clearly lack that particular Gate patina which gave them the glitter of success in the years at the Gaiety. In keeping with the mood of the forties they were not provocative; social comment was mainly confined to the superficial, gossipy chatter of arty circles with an occasional backward glance at the older pieties. MacLiammóir's last play, *Prelude in Kazbek Street*, was an exception. One critic described it as "the most sensitive and the most profound work on the theme of the homosexual's dilemma in the area of meaningful human relationships".[5] MacLiammóir wrote to Sally Travers:

> The title of my new play is found in the old Diaghilev Ballet called Tamar, whose castle was in the Pass of Kazbek — I think it's good but I am dubious about its appeal, as it is on an unpopular theme, and has no four-letter words and has no striptease.[6]

There was a muted response, the play's theme exciting no particular interest, and it was not revived. It is possible that the author had been too restrained for the mood of the times; Gay Rights activists were now rallying to tear down the walls of prejudice but MacLiammóir preferred the safe cameraderie of the ghetto within which he felt himself to be enclosed.

Most of MacLiammóir's plays were theatrical, in the best sense. He drew a clear distinction between drama as literature and drama as theatre; for this reason it is not surprising that only two of his plays were published: *Where Stars Walk* and the more frequently produced *Ill Met by Moonlight*. Set in the home of a Professor Sebastian Prosper, built within a fairy *rath* in Connemara, the latter play revolved around a folk-tale of a changeling. A newly-married bride disappears on May Eve and the changeling who takes her place is a possessed, evil creature who seduces, slanders and slays until she is exorcised by an old pishogue or charm. With Hilton Edwards as the Professor, Eithne Dunne as Catherine Mallaroe the changeling, and Maureen Cusack in a playful, elfin role, the whimsical affair was blended into an attractive mixture of modernity and melodrama. The author wrote for himself the bilingual part of a servant-boy who knows Irish and pretends to be in direct contact with the *sidhe* (fairies). The acting and the stylishness of the Gate decor once again captivated audiences.

In his next play, *Portrait of Miriam*, MacLiammóir turned away from the legendary past to tackle what at first sight seemed a contemporary theme. Using a device adopted by Thornton Wilder in *The Bridge of San Luis Rey*, he brought together a mixum-gatherum of characters — a priest, a poet, a soldier, a businessman and a light o' love — stranded for the night in a disused mansion. But by the end of the second act the audience was confronted with the familiar theme of the clash between the real and the unreal, the seen and the unseen. His old friend of the Abbey seance, A.J. Leventhal, reviewed *Portrait of Miriam* in the *Dublin Magazine*:

Micheál MacLiammóir must be counted among that rare band whose activities are essentially aesthetic and who must find expression in varying forms of art . . . . He is a romantic relying on fact and whimsy for the appeal of his early pictures and to make his plays pleasurably plausable.[7]

The Mountains Look Different was set in the West of Ireland and featured a woman of easy virtue who comes back from the big, bad city to disturb the rural simplicities and at least one simpleton. Unfortunately, the passion and the violence strained credibility as the play echoed with much of the melodramatic excess of an earlier era. MacLiammóir could never quite rid himself of a passion for "the noble lady Romanticism". He tells of her wonderful eyes seeing

> seas deluged with light, and awful forests full of darkness and mystery. Her robes are the colour of flame, and the hawk-eyed gods walk by her side, with enchanted rings upon her fingers. Her thoughts dwell with the gods and with the radiant and lovely creatures of her fancy, airy nameless creatures that never were and never could be except in the hallowed places which her mistress treads with her shining feet.[8]

Like most actor-playwrights, MacLiammóir's writing was influenced by playwrights whose work he had performed. Jean Anouilh helped to inspire the rather charming confection, *Slipper for the Moon*. A play within a pantomime — *Cinderella* — in which the author and Milo O'Shea played the Ugly Sisters, the piece proper told of the life of the pantomime cast offstage — the jealousies, the bickering, the romantic interludes and the heartbreak of separation. The spirit of pantomime is seen to survive not only in the make-believe of children but in the illusions of grown-ups. It was an ideal soufflé, like the earlier *Home for Christmas*, for a Gate Theatre audience; MacLiammóir was no Scrooge when seasonal fare was in demand.

In a revealing passage Hilton Edwards wrote briefly of Micheál's seventh talent as a musician. He could not read a score but, seated at a piano, he would transpose effortlessly into the keys he knew best — generally the romantic key of C. His plays resembled such improvisations, and were draped with the elegance of his costume design and settings. MacLiammóir eschewed naturalism as constrictive and destructive, believing with Gordon Craig that "it had never been the purpose of art to make uglier the ugliness of things, but to transform and make the already beautiful more beautiful, and in following this purpose art shields us with sweet influence from the dark sorrow of our weakness".[9]

Such ideas were anathema to the realist school of playwrights like Osborne, Wesker and Shelagh Delany, heralded by the critic Kenneth Tynan as the saviours of English theatre. Dialect was to become the norm for Shakespeare and the comedy of manners, if they were to be staged at all; Coward and even Wilde would have to wait for a decade or two more until the neo-naturalism of the post-war period had become as dated as the romanticism which had preceded it. But in this new era of realism the romantics, MacLiammóir and Edwards, were stranded. They showed no interest in Brendan Behan's first important play, *The Quare Fellow*, when it was submitted for production — there were no parts in that Ballad of Mountjoy Gaol which were of the remotest interest to either of them. The script lay about until Sally Travers read it and told Alan Simpson of its worth. He and Carolyn Swift rescued Behan's play from oblivion by staging it, not in the Gate, but in the tiny Pike Theatre in Herbert Lane.

The end of the war also brought back the English touring companies to the Gaiety and the Olympia. At this time, too, Irish actors and writers organized for better pay first in the Writers, Artists, Actors and Musicians Association and later in Irish Actors Equity. The part-time actors in the Gate and Abbey Companies expected to be paid as much as the full-time professionals who were earning between seven and ten pounds a week. Those who were paid less felt that they were regarded as amateurs and, with the security of steady day-jobs, they could afford to strike a hard bargain. This economic professionalism made it impossible for ambitious productions at the Gate, with big casts, to break even. Dublin theatre also saw a new diaspora of players as actors who could not travel abroad during the war years were now lured by offers of work in British films.

In 1947 the Gate Company toured to Belfast, Glasgow, London, Canada and New York where they staged *The Old Lady Says "No!"*, Shaw's *John Bull's Other Island*, *Ill Met by Moonlight*, *Where Stars Walk* and, in Canada only, *Portrait of Miriam*. The MacLiammóir plays were only moderately successful and foreign audiences found *The Old Lady Says "No!"* puzzling. Only wily old Shaw's fabulously sentimental Englishman, Broadbent (Hilton Edwards), duped by the silver-tongued but shrewder Irishman, Larry Doyle (MacLiammóir), made a lasting impression. It was neither a happy nor a successful return to America for MacLiammóir. The American critic, Mary McCarthy, unkindly suggested that he had chosen Dublin as his theatrical home so that he would be a bigger fish in a smaller pool. She had, evidently, never heard of the goldfish.

Like most leading men playing in repertory, on occasions MacLiammóir appeared in parts in which he bordered on self caricature. *Abdication*, by Mrs H. Lowe Porter, was billed as a chronicle play in the Shakespearean manner concerning a prince of royal blood (MacLiammóir) who renounces the throne to marry a commoner. It was clearly a pretentious parody of the Duke of Windsor's affair with Mrs Simpson. MacLiammóir emoted in the blankest of pseudo-Shakespearean verse and was so self-consciously graceful and regal that he seemed intent on showing the royals how they really ought to behave.

When MacLiammóir was not at ease in a part he had a tendency to gabble his lines and to stride about the stage, almost as if in search of an exit. He became over-emotional and stylized. But even as he approached his fiftieth year, MacLiammóir had the personal magnetism of the matinée idol. He sought and generally got the parts which he could adapt to his distinctive persona. The humdrum and the ordinary, the ungainly and the ugly aspects of the human condition were alien to MacLiammóir's temperament. Yet he could capture the tragic grandeur of an abject soul tottering on the brink; there was a demonic force within him that was both Apollonian and Dionysiac. He was much imitated but ultimately inimitable.

Most of those who got to know MacLiammóir realized that behind the camp and the romantic tinsel there was a generous and humble person. Though busy with both acting and writing, he was always ready to help a tyro. This writer was an assistant producer with *An Comhar Drámaíochta* whose plays in Irish MacLiammóir had directed in the early thirties. They were later brought under the aegis of the Abbey which announced a competition for a new play in Irish with a first prize of fifty pounds. I wrote a first draft of a play, *Ordóg an Bháis* (The Finger of Death) and asked MacLiammóir to read it. He not only read it but replied in October 1942:

I did like your play *Ordóg an Bháis* very much and would like to talk to you about it. The difficulty at the moment is the rush of work for our new season is at its feverish height and I can see no breathing space for a constructive talk for at least two weeks. Now here's a plan: would you keep your eyes on the bill and when you see *Emperor Jones* is on, would you write me and make a date for the theatre? I am only in a short play at the beginning and have the rest of the evening free. By, say, Wednesday of its week we could have an hour or two going over the MS in my dressing-room.

The short play was *The Man of Destiny* so I saw Mac-Liammóir as Napoleon on stage and then went backstage to his Gaiety dressing-room. He entered as if he were still on stage, standing for a moment in the doorway like Napolean on board the Bellerephon. After a second or two, he broke the spell with a low chuckling laugh as he warmly embraced some "darlings" who had rushed backstage to congratulate him. My compliments were brushed aside as mere *plámás*. It would be an understatement to say that he had stage presence; it was a penumbra which surrounded him wherever he went. Even when he spoke casually in conversational tone, it sounded conspiratorial and warmly intimate. There was always a sense of performance as if the delivery and timing of a trivial comment had been perfected by hours of private rehearsal. He seemed perfectly satisfied with an audience of one.

When the "fans" had gone, he had a brandy and a Gauloise cigarette, sending his over-attentive dresser to get me what I asked for — a bottle of stout. "*Buidéal leanna*" ordered Micheál although the poor fellow did not know a word of the language. There was no stage camp or facile gush as he got down to discussing the faults of my script in Irish so mellifluous that it softened the edge of his criticism. He insisted that he would read it again, this time noting his comments in the margin. He was as good as his word and in February 1943 he returned the play with an explanatory note:

Please forgive this letter being in English but my wicked secretary knows no Irish, and I am pressed for time. I am sending back your play which I really think on second reading has some fine stuff in it. Alas, I've only been able to show you what I mean in the first half of it, as work has been quite a nightmare lately, and I see no chance with our new season approaching of any slackening of pace.

With the help of his notes I rewrote the play and won the first prize in the competition.

MacLiammóir held great expectations for the potential of drama in Irish. He believed that the playwright who wrote in Irish was the inheritor of a new freedom which would allow him to break with naturalism and to throw off the shackles of what was called realism. Moreover, he would be free of the constraints imposed on the writer in English who is compelled, if he is to be staged, to give the public what it wants. Drama in Irish, MacLiammóir insisted, had as yet no public to dictate to playwrights. Thus they were free to shape the drama of the future in the theatre of the imagination — a symbolist drama free from the tyranny of the box-office and the box-set.

Dublin's boundless charity towards failure and its derisory dismissal of success had caught up with MacLiammóir and Edwards as they approached the half-century mark. They had become establishment figures of only slightly tarnished repute, no longer likely to man the barricades of the avant-garde with the fine frenzy of the thirties. Every new movement in theatre is a criticism of the movement immediately preceeding it or, as MacLiammóir put it, "the leaders of all new schools are betrayed by their disciples".

In the mid-forties new groups, usually headed by actors, rose and fell like ninepins. The Players Theatre, led by a group of dissenting Abbey actors with the high-minded and short-lived enthusiasm of youth, played a season at the Olympia. Shelah Richards, formerly of the Abbey and the Gate, put together a company which presented plays by Paul Vincent Caroll, Giradoux and O'Casey. Cyril Cusack formed a company which staged Shaw, Synge and one of the most controversial of the later O'Casey plays, *The Bishop's Bonfire*. This burgeoning of new theatre in Dublin meant that the Gaiety and Olympia Theatres were not as readily available to Edwards and Mac-Liammóir as they had been in earlier years while their real home, the Gate, available to them for only six months of each year, was an uneconomic proposition. The company was heavily in debt also, and so it was with some relief that MacLiammóir responded to a call in January 1949 from an early but unloved disciple, Orson Welles.

No Money in Thy Purse!

"The present, like a note of music, is nothing but as it appertains to what is past and what is to come."

Walter Savage Landor

ICHEÁL WAS IN bed recovering from "something the doctors called a nervous breakdown" but which he believed to be "possession by evil spirits" when the call came to play Iago. It was, he decided, a plot to get him out of bed. There was talk of a screen test in Paris — this was Shakespeare for the cinema — but then Welles decided that there was no need. He told Micheál that he was "made for the part" and added rather pointedly that Iago was impotent and that "the secret malady was, in fact, the keystone to the actor's approach".

MacLiammóir's *Put Money in Thy Purse — The Diary of the Film Othello* is a delightfully mischievous account of how Orson Welles made a picture with a maximum of panache and a minimum of money. It chronicles a crazy tour of Europe and North Africa — from Ireland to Paris, Rome, Marrakesh, Mogador, Safi, Casablanca; Paris and Rome again, then Venice, Marseilles and short interludes in Dublin and Belfast, all at the whim of the director who never seemed to know what or where he wanted to film next.

Orson wrote a preface to *Put Money in Thy Purse* in which he seemed reasonably satisfied with the diarist, with just one or two reservations:

He is an entertainer rather than a conquistador, a good companion, who could certainly scratch, but who prefers to purr. If he must be excluded from the full title of wit, his lack is ruthlessness and his only fault a preference for being kind.[1]

Welles protested more heatedly at his portrayal as "a rather unpalatable cocktail of Caliban, Pistol and Bottom, with an acrid whiff here and there of Coriolanus". He denied that he had railed and raged during rehearsals. On the contrary, he claimed that during almost every moment of their daily work Micheál was showered "with highly merited praise". And he was at pains to point out that he never called Micheál "harp".

"Harp", you see, brings to mind that improbable figure, the Irish-American of St Patrick's Day parades, complete with budget-sized shamrocks and souvenir shillelagh, and Micheál is something else again. His far-wandering spirit has chosen never to travel without a plush knapsack, plum-coloured and chock-full of the more attractive Edwardian airs and continental graces, but no shamrocks at all. Indeed Micheál, who does really look a bit like something Beardsley would have drawn if they'd taken away his pencil-sharpener, is the very last Irishman on the broad face of the earth to be called "harp".[2]

If the director and his leading man failed to find words adequate for one another off the set, filming was not without some gaps in communication too. Often, when the cast was ready, the costumes were not; when the costumes arrived, one or more of the cast was missing. While in Mogador, in June 1949, there were no costumes for Cassio and Roderigo. Iago's attempted murder of Cassio and actual murder of Roderigo was to take place on the street but, in the absence of costumes, Orson decided to film the scene in a Turkish bath. So Dublin-born actor Michael Laurence (formerly Clarke), who played Cassio, and the English actor Bob Coote, as Roderigo, appeared "stripped and draped and turbaned in towels".

> Action then proceeds through comedy scene of Iago's instructions about the murder of Cassio to series of shots in crooked stone passages and wash-rooms hung with dripping towels and full of vague shapes of bathers and of negro masseurs carrying jars of oil and vats of boiling water through clouds of vapour. Bob (in *negligé*) and me (in leather tunic) plotting and peering through ominous gratings and barred windows at Cassio being massaged while I hiss "It makes us or it mars us, think of that" . . .[3]

MacLiammóir found Welles's improvisation "effective and ingenious", adding that "it will certainly save much bacon".

Off the set he discussed "Berlin before Hitler, Stage before Cinema, and Orson before Othello to say nothing of Othello before Orson".[4] Hilton arrived to play Brabantio. There were Lucullan feasts in luxury hotels and local fare in bistros and low dives as the film was slowly completed, in short takes, until money and the patience of the cast ran out. It was all as exotic as the Thousand and One Nights — the unexpurgated version —

until, after the vapours of the Venetian lagoons, a tired and exhausted Iago was dragged through the streets of Mogador in a dog collar. All the time Orson bullied, bellowed and cajoled, insisting on take after take, shouting at times, "Now, now, Ireland's answer to Nijinsky, let's do it again".

On 7 March 1950 it was with immense relief that Micheál heard Orson say, "Mr MacLiammóir, I am happy to tell you that you are now an out-of-work actor. You have finished Iago."

There was worse news to come, though. Welles owed MacLiammóir some £2,000 for arrears of salary. Still more seriously, some damage had been done to his sight because he had not been warned of the danger of looking into strong searchlights improvised by Welles for the shooting of some of the scenes. After finishing Othello, Welles asked MacLiammóir and Edwards to collaborate with him in the staging of his own version of Marlowe's *Doctor Faustus* and in a new play he had written about Hollywood, *The Unthinking Lobster*. Both plays opened in Paris in June 1950 with Edwards playing Mephistopheles to Welles's Faustus. Welles made an unlikely choice for Helen — "the face that launched a thousand ships" — in Eartha Kitt, an unknown black beauty whom he had discovered in "a highly sophisticated night-club run by a lesbian". It was arranged that MacLiammóir would replace Edwards during a tour of Germany, but by now Micheál had taken flight.

Welles took a belated revenge. In the book based on his interviews with Barbara Leaming he departed from the relatively amiable if sometimes barbed wit that had characterised many of his earlier remarks and departed, too, from the spirit of his preface to *Put Money in Thy Purse*. With his subject safely dead, he gave lurid descriptions of a series of MacLiammóir's alleged encounters with gondoliers and Arab policemen.

Micheál MacLiammóir had left Paris to adjudicate at a rural amateur drama festival in Ireland, demonstrating priorities that Welles was unable to understand. The organizers of the Kerry Drama Festival, from their point of view, were delighted to have succeeded in engaging MacLiammóir as an adjudicator at their competition in Killarney. The amateur movement was then only beginning to make an impact in rural Ireland, and the presence of this pre-eminent figure in the professional theatre came as a welcome boost in confidence to those at the festival in Killarney.

On the opening night of the festival MacLiammóir spoke in fluent Irish and displayed a fine knowledge of the Kerry poets whose monument stood near his hotel. He proved to be sympathetic and considerate to everybody except garrulous American tourists and gabbling English women. To the untutored players, he was kindness itself; there was no trace of superiority in his attitude: rather, he took very seriously his role as adjudicator.

Paul Vincent Carroll's *Shadow and Substance* to-night. Not I fear very well done. Found I can't be too hard on them! No people who are trying to do anything at all should meet with discouragement in this land of ruin and need. One must tell the truth, but one should in the manner of a tactful dentist with his wheel, go gently. Every illusion one takes from the searcher must be replaced by an image of truth, if indeed one can find it oneself. This country teems with aesthetic misfortune, with talented individuals incapable of an hour of work, with conceited jackanapes who imagine they are artists because they'd like to be, with pompous incompetent critics who fatuously praise or indiscriminately rend and who are themselves more ignorant of their subject than the ignorance they attack . . . . Unconstructive criticism even of amateurs (who don't matter except that they may be, and probably are hatching among them an individual talent that will one day matter very much) is a form of murder as surely as the fulsome flattery with which the amateur is faced as an alternative is a form of seduction of the young. In the case of a bad show, I'd rather be dumb than guilty.[5]

Offstage he talked to everybody, dined with some of the local clergy and went for long walks late at night on the lakeshore with the gentle chairman of the Festival, Donnchadh Ó Sé. There were motor-trips by day to Slea Head with Festival secretary Mary Leane and Robin Hilliard, a local merchant.

In an interview in the *Kerryman* he spoke in favour of the setting-up of an All-Ireland Drama Festival and said that he "would like to see writers at various centres given a chance by the producers to try out their plays on the stage". Three years later the first All-Ireland Drama Festival was held in Athlone, and before the decade was out the Listowel Drama Group's production of *Sive*, by local author John B. Keane (whom Mac-Liammóir described as the Douanier Rousseau of the Irish theatre) marked a turning point in Irish drama.

From Killarney MacLiammóir returned to Paris where he took over from Edwards in *Doctor Faustus* for a disastrous tour of Germany. On the tour Welles decided to include a potted version of *The Importance of Being Earnest* without a Lady Bracknell; the show ended up, much to Micheál's disgust, as "An Evening with Orson Welles". He even did conjuring tricks during the intervals while Eartha Kitt filled in with Duke Ellington numbers. Germany, however, had lost interest in an actor whom they knew only as Harry Lime in *The Third Man*. Welles went to London to play *Othello* on stage at the St James Theatre, under the direction of Sir Laurence Olivier. The Australian actor, Peter Finch, played Iago. It was a humiliation which MacLiammóir had to suffer in silence. Welles's film of *Othello* was acclaimed by the critics and voted the joint-winner of the Grand Prix at the Cannes Film Festival in 1952, but the commercial cinemas showed little interest and there were distribution problems in the States. MacLiammóir's chance of being paid for his part in the film receded further.

On their return to Dublin MacLiammóir and Edwards found that the Gate Theatre Company was in dire straits. In 1944 the partners had purchased a fine Regency house at 4 Harcourt Terrace with a pleasant, brick-walled garden at the rear; now the house and its contents were mortgaged to shore up the declining fortunes of the Gate. Although MacLiammóir had little money he was never in those years really poor: like Oscar Wilde, he had a high standard of destitution. Edwards, who was inclined to be a big spender, put pressure on Welles to make some effort to clear his debt. Welles obliged by making a brief appearance, for no fee, in a moderately successful film, *Return to Glenascaul*, which was directed by Hilton Edwards. In a brief scene in which he was driving in the Dublin mountains, Welles came across another motorist whose car had broken down. Rolling down his window, he asked, "Something wrong?"

"I'm having trouble with my distributor," replied the other driver.

"So am I," ad libbed Orson as he drove off, thinking of his losses on *Othello*.

In another payment in kind MacLiammóir, on the recommendation of Welles, was given the part of Edgar in an American television production of *King Lear* with Welles in the title role. Welles usually showed more interest in Hilton Edwards' work than in MacLiammóir's and he came back to Dublin to see him in *Death of a Salesman*, a play in which MacLiammóir had no part. On a visit to the Gate in 1952 to see *Tolka* Row Welles was heckled by an angry picket from the self-appointed Catholic Cinema and Theatre Patron's Association who, as a result of Senator Joe McCarthy's witch-hunt in the States, believed that Welles was a communist. Hilton Edwards remarked to the demonstrators that, as far as he could judge, Welles had spent most of his life trying unsuccessfully to be a capitalist.

With one or two exceptions, most of the shows staged in the Gate in the early fifties plunged the company deeper into debt. A welcome invitation in 1952 to stage *Hamlet* in the courtyard of Kronberg Castle at Elsinore, Denmark, was regarded as a belated tribute to MacLiammóir's prowess. To adjust to the open-air conditions at Elsinore Edwards experimented with a partly Elizabethan style in an effort to overcome the problems of staging the play on a large platform. Lighting, as he had previously handled it, had to go. Costumes were more Jacobean and the background consisted of moveable panels. There were no front curtains.

Rain and hail all but swamped the Elsinore performance. Attendants, at intervals, scattered sawdust on the platform stage. These were testing conditions for MacLiammóir who, more like Lear than Hamlet, bellowed against the elements. His predecessors at Elsinore, Laurence Olivier, John Gielgud and the Finnish actor, Erik Lindstrom, had all been much younger when they had appeared there. At fifty-three years of age MacLiammóir's bravura approach could not overcome the wind and the rain. The production was respectfully but not enthusiastically received, while the harshest of the Danish critics dismissed it as "the Hamlet of an old-age pensioner".

The Elsinore *Hamlet* was staged at the Olympia Theatre, Dublin, in July 1952 and on the first night MacLiammóir announced that it would be his farewell appearance in the part. This was something that the great actors of his youth, such as McMaster, would not have even considered, but the days when the great leading roles — apart from Lear — were played by actors over fifty were coming to an end. The invasion of the theatre by cinema and television ordained that an actor had to look the part before he played it. MacLiammóir seemed reconciled to this fact when he agreed to play King Claudius opposite Cyril Cusack's Hamlet at the Gaiety in 1957. It was directed by an American, Howard Sackler, who was strongly influenced by Cusack's approach to the play. Cusack, an actor who seldom failed to bring his own distinctive, precise interpretation to every part he played, gave a quirky, edgy performance; his interpretation lacked what Leigh Hunt aptly called "the royal warrant". MacLiammóir, still hurt by the Elsinore debacle, petulantly dismissed Cusack's Hamlet as "the Prince of Denmark Street" — a reference to an obscure Dublin thoroughfare.

MacLiammóir now saw many of the parts in which he had excelled entrusted to younger actors. Even some of the parts which he had created in his own plays were being performed by a young actor, Patrick Bedford, whom Hilton Edwards had groomed for leading roles. Bedford played many of the juvenile leads during the 1956 tour to Egypt and Malta with a repertoire which included Anouilh's *The Lark* and *Ring Round the Moon*, *The Picture of Dorian Gray* and *The*

Merchant of Venice. Eithne Dunne, who had weathered the storm as Ophelia at Elsinore, gave splendid performances, particularly in *The Lark*. The spotlight was focused on new stars. In the Gate productions of the early fifties, Siobhán McKenna scored a personal triumph in Shaw's *Saint Joan* in which Mac-Liammóir was a fine Earl of Warwick and Jack MacGowran an excellent Dauphin. But when Brendan Smith, the Dublin Theatre Festival impressario, brought the production to Paris a few years later, MacLiammóir unwisely took on the part of the Dauphin. He could not and did not want to look as MacGowran had, exactly as Shaw described: "he has narrow little eyes, near together, a long pendulous nose that droops over his short upper lip, and the expression of a young dog accustomed to being kicked, yet incorrigible and irrepressible". MacLiammóir appeared more like an overweight French poodle.

New stage designers like Carl Bonn, Michael O'Herlihy and a brilliant Scot, Molly McEwen, did the work which had been MacLiammóir's sole responsibility in earlier decades. Edwards, his partner, directed the new and successful Globe Theatre Company in Paul Vincent Carroll's *The Wayward Saint* and also worked for independent producers like Stephen Held and P.J. O'Connor who staged *Mother Courage*. For a modern dress *Julius Caesar* in 1957 the Gate Company joined forces with Anew McMaster's company; MacLiammóir was an impassioned Mark Antony and McMaster an impressive Brutus. But newspaper headlines like "Caesar Arrives In Jet Plane" did not succeed in bringing great crowds to the Gaiety.

An exception to this temporary eclipse was MacLiammóir's splendid performance at the Gate in the title role of Pirandello's *Henry IV*. During a medieval pageant taking place in a modern Italian town, an actor playing Henry IV, Emperor of the Holy Roman Empire, falls from his horse and hits his head on a stone; when he recovers from the blow he believes himself to be the monarch he was playing. In his temporary insanity he recreates the imperial court with courtiers and vassals attired in eleventh-century costume — the long-dead Emperor lives again in the actor's imagination. And even when sanity returns the man opts for the dream-world, rather than return to the real world, preferring "the reality of madness". In a virtuoso performance MacLiammóir recreated this masquerade of the past with the same assurance he had shown in projecting Emmet into the twentieth century in *The Old Lady Says "No!"*.

MacLiammóir gave a farewell performance in that play by Denis Johnston when the Gate Company joined with Longford Productions for a Dublin Theatre Festival production in 1957. He described this last appearance in the role of the Speaker/ Emmet as *noche triste, noche fatal*. The joint-venture with Longford Productions did not end old animosities. The internal arrangement at the Gate whereby both companies had alternate seasons had worked reasonably well, but that year Dublin Corporation insisted on further renovations to comply with more stringent safety regulations. It was left to Lord Longford to raise most of the money by public subscription or from his own, seemingly inexhaustible purse. On Lord Longford's death in 1961, MacLiammóir wrote to Ulick O'Connor that "the death of an enemy seems more distressing than that of a friend". In a way, this was a bleak, distressing truth.

For some years Ulick O'Connor had been drama critic of *Dublin Opinion* and his reviews of MacLiammóir's perfor-mances greatly pleased the actor who had come to believe that "this is no country for an actor over twenty-five. Ireland mistrusts maturity." In a letter inviting O'Connor to lunch in 1954, he wrote:

> I was born with a minimum sense of guilt and the one thing that stirs it to a pleasurable conscious (*sic*) is having lunch with a critic . . . so that if anyone tells you about Micheál being always the same you can tell them with great wistful humility from me that I am indeed sad if I'm the same in *Hamlet* and *Carmen Miranda* or in *Tolka Row* and *Richard II*.

MacLiammóir played all roles, from tragedy to pantomime. Years earlier in Christmas shows at the Gate, his female imper-sonations were greatly admired and now, in order to put money in his purse, he was engaged by Louis Elliman for pantomime and revues at the Gaiety. There he had to match his comic talent against the unrivalled comedian, Jimmy O'Dea. In a revue sketch O'Dea and MacLiammóir impersonated one another, Micheál playing Jimmy and Jimmy playing Micheál. In another show, MacLiammóir rhumba'd his way as Carmen Miranda and did an outrageous take-off of Ireland's only prima donna, Margaret Burke Sheridan. Maggie from Mayo, as she liked to call herself, would speak in Italian or French to anyone she met provided she was sure they did not know either language. In MacLiammóir's sketch she appeared as Madame Phenobarbitone, speaking three or four languages all mixed up together. His impersonations of a Cork shawlie or a Paris Madame were as wicked as they were accurate, and again he teamed up with Milo O'Shea to play the Ugly Sisters in *Cinderella*.

But MacLiammóir did not really relish the rough and tumble of pantomime, with its flying scenery and complicated machinery; he nearly had a serious accident while playing King Rat in *The Pied Piper* at the Gaiety. MacLiammóir demonstrated considerable versatility in his acting when pressed by economic circumstances to seek whatever work was available; he took part, with Anew McMaster, in a pageant about Saint Patrick which was staged in the wide open spaces of Croke Park. However, things were at a low ebb when MacLiammóir joined his friend Anton Dolin for a children's show, *Where the Rainbow Ends*, in London at Christmas 1957. Only the ballet scenes with the children appealed to him. A part in a forgotten play, *The Key Above the Door*, added to his dejection. He wrote home:

We're playing Streatham this week. Hilton is here preparing a play for the Gaiety — not our management, he's doing it for Louis [Elliman]. We both hate our life at the moment. It's all so formless and unlike what we had planned and still hope for; but Dublin is really a difficult place for the theatre and seems from all I hear less and less inclined for anything — outside ballet and opera — but pantomime and revue. If there was a living to be earned we'd be back tomorrow —

today. I still hope to find a way. I don't think the Irish papers are wildly interested at the moment in Hilton or me — and there's no reason why they should be.[6]

More in sorrow than in anger, MacLiammóir felt neglected and excluded from the charmed circle within which he wanted to shine. Even at his most successful as a designer and playwright, he had felt that his proper place in the theatre was as an actor playing the most coveted roles. Some half a dozen of his performances in the thirties and forties had set him apart from most of his contemporaries, at least in Ireland. He was at his best in romantic and heroic roles and from his earliest years with McMaster had excelled in Shakespeare. His narcissism in no way diminished his impact on an audience; in Hilton Edwards' phrase, he was never the kind of Lorenzo who really wanted to play Jessica.

There were critics, at home and abroad, who dismissed MacLiammóir's style as a pose, a throw-back to the grand manner of the Victorian era. In fact, his approach to acting had much more in common with the sophisticated artificiality of the twenties; he could switch easily from mannered comedy to classical tragedy. Yet he believed that stage acting, as distinct from acting in films, should be unreservedly theatrical. Like his partner, he regarded what was described as naturalistic acting as just one other convention which the theatre had at its disposal. In acting, just as in settings and decor, realism had its limitations when compared with the resources of the cinema and television. For this reason he could not easily adjust to the colloquial, vernacular dialogue and the social realism of the new playwrights of the fifties. He once told Sally Travers that he "could be natural" but that it was "a very difficult pose to keep up".

While still a comparatively young man, Yeats had honoured him with the accolade: "You are a magnificent actor", and MacLiammóir was certainly not one of the tribe the poet dismissed contemptuously in the lines:[7]

But actors lacking music
Do most excite my spleen,

They say it is more human
To shuffle grunt and groan,
Not knowing what unearthly stuff
Rounds a mighty scene.

For MacLiammóir great acting was a thing of the spirit. He tried to create out of the innermost recesses of his being; his search was within himself for that elusive quality which made a great part distinctly his own. This mysterious alchemy was accompanied by a precision of technique which he described brilliantly:

To be an actor demands a curious and complete surrender of the self and of many personal claims, and I reflected how all art is a wrestling match with life, and how acting more than any other art is a demonstration of rebellion against the mundanity of everyday existence. Far from being a copyist of life's surface tricks or a facile repeater of traditional antics, the actor should live with such delicacy, with such intensity, that he brings manner and style to all the unimportant trifles of gesture and speech, so that the eating of a fruit, the folding of a letter, the raising of the arm, the donning of a cap, all become in his hands images of significance, profound mirrors of character. To act is to live for a moment with an intenser life, to pass bodily into the sphere of sorrows and of joys greater than our own, to thrust the shoddy surface of what we call real life upwards to a transforming radiance; and while the painter must see and the poet and the musician hear with passion before they hurry to canvas or to paper and ink, the actor must note all down with calmness and precision and must then give to the single moment everything he possesses, soul and voice and body, the inner and outer selves.[8]

MacLiammóir went to the United States in 1959 to play Don Pedro in *Much Ado About Nothing* directed by Sir John Gielgud. It seemed that Dublin had little more to offer him. There were critics who felt that he might be a more disciplined and less indulgent actor if he were to make a complete break with the city of his adoption and the fulsome flattery of some of the local reviewers. His performances on an international tour in 1954 as Judge Brack in *Hedda Gabler* and in an Edinburgh Festival production of Jonathan Griffin's *The Hidden King* in 1957 had been acclaimed by audiences that knew little of his Dublin fame.

In an effort to clear the Gate Company's debts, Hilton Edwards put his trust in Orson Welles's star quality in a proposed Shakespearean presentation in which Welles would play Falstaff in scenes from *Henry IV*, *Henry V* and *The Merry Wives of Windsor*. After interminable delays *Chimes at Midnight*, billed as the adventures of the fat knight and the Prince of Wales from the historical plays of William Shakespeare, opened at the Belfast Grand Opera House, on 13 February 1960, and after a week transferred to the Gaiety Theatre, Dublin. The English actor Keith Baxter played Prince Hal and, once again, MacLiammóir had no part. He was put off with a vague promise by Welles of a part in a London production of the *Duchess of Malfi* which never materialized. *Chimes at Midnight* was a box-office flop and Welles left Dublin for the last time owing more money than ever not only to Edwards and MacLiammóir but also to the astute Gaiety manager Louis Elliman.

Elliman was less than enthusiastic when a diffident MacLiammóir first mentioned the possibility of his one-man show on Wilde: if Orson Welles could not fill the Gaiety in a starring role, who could? The theatre manager reluctantly agreed, but insisted that if MacLiammóir was to do a one-man show, it would have to wait until the Dublin Theatre Festival in the autumn, when the Gaiety would have a guarantee against loss from the Festival funds. After a decade of doubt and disillusion, MacLiammóir got his chance to demonstrate the Importance of Being Micheál.

· X ·

The Reingreencarnation

Life is a long rehearsal for a play that is never produced.

Micheál MacLiammóir *All for Hecuba*

THE SUGGESTION THAT MacLiammóir should present a one-man show with Oscar Wilde as its subject had first been made by London producer Peter Ashmore in 1954. In Amsterdam on tour with *Hedda Gabler* — a memorable production starring Peggy Ashcroft, in which MacLiammóir played an impressive Judge Brack — Peter Ashmore put it to him as they talked over dinner in a restaurant on the Rembrandtsplein. MacLiammóir had earlier expressed an aversion to the notion of performing one-man shows, suggesting that they were the prerogative of women of genius such as Ruth Draper. But with the assistance of generous amounts of yellow chartreuse the persistent Peter Ashmore succeeded in dispelling his resistance. They parted "with mutual esteem and the profound sobriety of the semi-intoxicated", and Micheál soon began to contemplate seriously the creation of a one-man show.

As he contemplated the likely form and content of the enterprise other doubts came to haunt him, doubts which had to do with the choice of Wilde as subject. For lurking in his memories of an Edwardian childhood were evasive and uneasy conversations between a father and his young son:

"What was wrong about Oscar Wilde?"

"What's that?" my father said.

I repeated the question.

After ambiguities and non-sequiturs about Wilde's brilliance, his books and his badness, an exasperated father blurted out something "he had heard or read somewhere":

"The man Wilde was guilty of a far greater sin, God forgive him, than the sin of going to bed with bad women. He turned young men into women."

Like Stephen Dedalus after the Hell Fire sermon at Clongowes Wood College, MacLiammóir's young mind was disturbed:

I remember no more of the conversation, because at my father's last words, my brain caught fire. Before my eyes a magician arose, from a sea of clouds black as Acheron, irresistibly smiling: a dim, terrifying figure swathed in scarlet, wielding a wand like some monstrous being in a pantomime, a sorcerer at whose bidding all things were changed. And this horror, this ogre, yet was smiling: he was grand and gay and witty and good natured. . . . Ah! what sort of Titan confronted me here? A shadow, monstrous, laughing, insolent, dark and radiant as Lucifer himself, *turning men into women*. His very name was spotted like an orchid.

Oscar, oscurillous, oscar-faced, oscarlet, oscarrion . . . our monuments shall be the maws of kites . . . Oscariot! Oscar Wilde . . . the lips pursed forward to pronounce the petulant "W" of Wildeness, wilderness, of wilful witchcraft, of wanton wickedness . . . Oscar Wilde.[1]

MacLiammóir claimed that he never consciously chose Oscar Wilde as an exemplar nor saw him as a direct influence on his own life and behaviour. He could never quite accept Wilde's uncontrolled passion for youth which he found "depressingly elderly; a dear old gentleman drooling over a hockey team". MacLiammóir could never be accused of the corruption of young men, and he well realized that it was this wilful passion for "rose-coloured youth" that had, together with his inordinate hatred of the Marquis of Queensberry, landed Oscar Wilde in jail. But as a subject Wilde proved irresistible.

He prepared a draft script after re-reading nearly everything that had been written by or about Wilde. Robert Sherard, Arthur Ransome, André Gide, Vincent O'Sullivan, Hesketh Pearson, even Frank Harris, all had parts in the original text which, unassisted by the voice of the interpreter/narrator, read as something of a hotch-potch. Hilton Edwards appraised the result with a mixture of wit and sarcasm:

"Oh, I know how real he is to you," Hilton demurred, "But kindly remember that your business is to make him real to your audience not just to wallow in the company of a ghost.

"It's going to be much too long," Hilton continued, "Much too long and the great thing will be to leave them wanting more. Yet I don't know — it's all good stuff. . . . And I like the links you are writing too; but you are up to your old tricks again of course. Never use one adjective when five will do; that's your motto. . . . Oscar, himself, is at his weakest when he uses too many, and at his best when a line comes out like a pistol shot."

Hilton fired shots in several directions, but one at least hit the target:

"Mind you, I do not like the idea of you trying to *look* like him at all really. I don't see you holding any audience for a whole first act with greenery-yallery. False nose too if it's to be convincing: he had a Roman nose, didn't he? You and your abbreviated Gipsy snout."

"Ach," I said, suddenly tired of it all: I have not Hilton's power of burning concentration on one subject over an unlimited time. "I don't think I'd better do it at all."

"There you go," he answered. "Irish people. Oh my God! No stamina you see. *No stamina*. Now shut up for a moment: let me think: . . . Do it as yourself, . . . As yourself! Are you listening? A dinner jacket. Yourself. A recital, not a play. But don't bill it as a recital. Fundamentally, it will be an entertainment. But we can't call it that either." [2]

This led to a long battle of words about what to call it: "Rise and Fall of an Aesthete", "The Green Carnation", "The Happy Prince", "Sunflowers and Broad Arrows", "From Merrion Square to Reading Gaol".

And then one morning as I lay supine in the bath and Hilton in pajama trousers, whirling in and out and brandishing a shaving brush, still (even at that hour of the morning) hot on the trail of myriad new suggestions, I, in the exasperation of sheer reactionary boredom, suddenly rebelled and shouted:

"Is a title of such importance?"

"Wilde thought so. He had Importance on the brain: *Women of No Importance, Importance of Being Earnest* . . ."

"Well call it *The Importance of Being Wilde*, for God's sake," I told him, "and let me get out of the bath!"

Suddenly, Hilton ceased to wheel and whirl, "Not bad, not bad."

"What's not bad," I asked, wrenching myself free from the water and reaching for a towel.

"*The Importance of Being Wilde* — that's it. That's it! But the rhythm's faulty. It ought to be the same."

"As what?"

Such futile questioning was ignored.

"One syllable's no good, don't you see that? It should have two. It *must* have two. That's my talc you are using. Not that I mind in the least: God knows, you're welcome to anything I have. But you won't put it back. I know you. Age cannot wither nor custom stale your infinite kleptomania. You're hell to work with anyway. No concentration. Never did have. Your Lorca fandangos have no effect on me at all. *Two* syllables. It's essential."

"I don't know what you are talking about."

"*Earnest*, of course, Oh my God! *Wilde*, No, no; obviously. I've got it, I've got it! *Importance of Being Oscar*."

"*THE Importance of Being Oscar*," I corrected him. It was the only way to preserve any dignity at all.[3]

As work on the show continued, MacLiammóir felt a sense of foreboding at the prospect of being alone on the stage for several hours. His consolation was that he would not be quite alone. "There would be the audience," he mused, adding with mock modesty, "They were the one hope: if they came in at all." Popular reaction amongst Dublin's theatregoers, once news of the impending production became known, was decidedly favourable. "Is it MacLiammóir as Oscar? Isn't he playing the part all the days of his life?" They neither knew nor cared that an actor of MacLiammóir's sensibility dies a death, as the saying goes, on every first night. They were unaware, too, of the years of contemplation and months of preparation which had gone into this one-man show, which promised to be part-catharsis, part-exorcism for the sixty-year-old actor. Gradually he yielded to the enchantment of having a stage to himself without the distraction of interruptions by any other player. Then nothing but a total blackout or a backstage epidemic could prevent him from experiencing the exhilaration of being alone with an audience and "with God — or with the devil, whichever happened that night to be in one's heart".

On the first night at the Gaiety he responded admirably to Hilton Edwards' direction. In the first half of the show he summoned on stage with seemingly effortless spontaneity such diverse characters as Lord Goring, Lord Henry Wotten, Dorian Gray, Mr John Worthing, Lady Bracknell and even Salomé in the original French.

The one interval in the performance encompassed the period of the trials of Oscar Wilde and the second part opened with the announcement of his sentence to two years' hard labour. The lilies of the opening scene are replaced by sere and yellow leaves as the shadows close in on the doomed man, now slowly dying, as he said, beyond his means. There are long passages from *De Profundis*, and *The Ballad of Reading Gaol* is for once recited in its entirety. But despite the tragic fall the irresistible gaiety of Wilde survives to the curtain line when the dying Oscar whispers to his great friend Robert Ross: "Robbie — when the last trumpet sounds and you and I are couched in our purple and porphyry tombs, I shall turn and whisper to you: 'The Last Trumpet!' But oh Robbie, I shall add, 'Robbie, dear boy, let us pretend we do not hear it.'"

He had one unpleasant experience, early in the run of the show, when an elderly dowager in a box, looking as formidable as Lady Bracknell, heckled frequently, saying that she was "a cousin of Lord Alfred Douglas, the great poet and perfect gentleman whom Oscar Wilde destroyed". Like Robbie at Oscar's bedside, MacLiammóir pretended not to hear and the Gorgon was shushed into silence.

His polished delivery of his own linking commentary had touches of Wilde's own brilliance:

Aesthetically speaking, Oscar Wilde, I seriously suggest to you, invented the period we speak of today as the 1890s, through the first half of which famous decade he strutted and through the second half of which he staggered . . .

The Nineties of the Green Carnation were dead and gone forever: the mood of the Yellow Book was to make way for the reign of the Yellow Press. . . . Anything you disapproved of you said was Unwholesome and you snorted. If, however, you were the sort of person who did approve of that sort of thing, you said it was "deciduously exotic", and you breathed through your nose. So you see people haven't changed at all really: only things like hats and adjectives change . . . [4]

The Dublin newspaper critics shouted one another down with superlatives. The severest comment was that the curtain had not come down until after midnight but it seemed that missed buses mattered little and that late deadlines were the hallmark of greatness. MacLiammóir expressed delight, embarrassment and boredom in equal measures. He realized that reviews were of only ephemeral significance and disapproved thoroughly of actors who quoted their favourite press notices long after everybody else, including the critics who wrote them, had forgotten all about them. On the rare occasions when he was slated by a critic he kept the cutting for a while in his wallet and read it to amuse admirers at parties.

A review in the London *Times* by Ulick O'Connor was, however, of particular significance, for it prompted Sir Michael Redgrave and Fred Sadoff to bring the show to London for a limited run at the Apollo Theatre. Before it transferred to the Royal Court Theatre the management insisted on a cut of forty minutes playing time; the painful surgery was performed by Emlyn Williams, and Micheál had to bid farewell to Oscar's comments on Ellen Terry and Sir Henry Irving, to chunks of Dorian Gray and — the unkindest cut of all — several verses from *The Ballad of Reading Gaol*. His seasons at both the Apollo and the Royal Court were received with almost unqualified praise by the London critics. The *Daily Express* reviewer was completely captivated:

Genius meets genius . . . it is an explosion of incomparable richness, boldness, passion and beauty. As I left they were just starting to cheer. I daresay they are cheering still.

The *Evening Standard* indulged in prophecy:
The day will come when your stage-struck children will ask if you ever saw the greatest of Irish actors, Micheál MacLiammóir, impersonate Oscar Wilde. I would not want you to say "No".

From New York came an invitation from Sol Hurok to play at the Lyceum Theatre in the spring of 1961. Before this New York date he had another, six-week run at the Gaiety in Dublin.

Louis Elliman, no longer a doubting Thomas, arranged an on-stage celebration on the last night of the run. "An Oscar for an Oscar," he called it. The critic Gabriel Fallon lined up seven distinguished Irishmen to wish Micheál *bon voyage* and to present him with a piece of Waterford Glass. Ernest Blythe represented the Abbey Theatre and Cathal O'Shannon, journalist and Labour Court member, spoke as "an inveterate theatregoer". Commenting on the performance, Cathal wryly remarked: "Ernest Blythe and myself got a bit sentimental about *The Ballad of Reading Gaol* because we were both there for a while, though not in Oscar's time and not for the same reason". Micheál described the affair as

"a more pleasant version of TV's *This Is Your Life* which, with respect to my friend Eamonn Andrews, is a barbarous institution, to bring on elderly gentlemen like us and say 'This is your Godmother whom we have flown home from Australia!'"

And Dubliners, he reminded the audience, are never so happy as when they hear you are going away and give you an "Isn't that great that you're going to the States" send-off.

In New York the critics responded to *The Importance of Being Oscar* like tipsy uncles at a birthday party: they raved about everything. The *New York Herald Tribune*'s critic "found magic at every turn of the wheel". Howard Taubman wrote in the *New York Times*:

It is a virtuoso performance.... But even as he performs, Mr MacLiammóir preserves a strong measure of his own identity.

Unlike other one-man shows devoted to recalling the person and creative world of a renowned writer, Mr MacLiammóir does not attempt to assume his subject's appearance . . .

The shadows close in as the first half ends . . . when he returns the lilies in the case have been replaced by trailing autumn leaves. Mr MacLiammóir himself stands in a sombre half-light, his head bowed like a man who has been through purgatory. . . . He is an Irishman proudly proclaiming a compatriot's expression, in himself and in his work, of the spirit of Ireland.

· XI ·

Our Revels Now Are Ended

"If one tells the truth one is sure, sooner or later, to be found out."

Oscar Wilde

PRAISE DID NOT translate into box-office success at a New York theatre that people told him was too large but the reputation of his one-man show led to further invitations to tour, first across the States, and then to Rio de Janeiro, Bogota and other cities in South America, where he drew big houses.

In 1961 MacLiammóir played *The Importance of Being Oscar* at the Theatre du Vieux Colombier in Paris, the city in which, he confessed, he would have loved to have been acclaimed as "a new exotically combined edition of Sacha Guitry and Monet Sully". But playing *Salomé* in the French original only begged the question for a Paris audience as to why the performance was not all in French. Even the more literary minded critics did not seem to empathize with Wilde's tragic end in the Hotel d'Alsace. They had martyrs enough of their own, for no sooner had literature been acknowledged as a profession in post-revolutionary Paris than it had thrown up more than its share of tragedies. The shores of French poesy are strewn with the wrecks: Gerard de Nerval, Baudelaire, Villiers de l'Isle Adam, Verlaine . . . If their gorgeous dreams had not sustained them, what sympathy was left for Wilde? A monument in Père Lachaise, of course! But to the jaded French intellectual Oscar Wilde and MacLiammóir's summoning up of his spirit seemed as faded as the covers of the *Yellow Book*.

In April 1962 he appeared in Dublin at the Gaiety Theatre in a "midnight matinée" performed as a tribute to the stage-manager Tom Jones. Billed as *Stars at Midnight*, there were three solo performances by Peter Ustinov, Anew MacMaster and Micheál MacLiammóir. Micheál presented excerpts from famous Irish writers, from the probably mythical Amergin to the decidedly real James Joyce.

After MacLiammóir's *Stars at Midnight* appearance with McMaster, it was planned that they would appear together in a Dublin Theatre Festival production of *Othello*. McMaster became gravely ill during rehearsals and died on 24 August 1962. MacLiammóir played Iago to William Marshall's Othello for one week at the Gaiety and later in Antwerp, Brussels and the Hague. His Iago, like his grief at McMaster's passing, seemed muted. He believed in grieving not for the dead but for those who were left behind, and in this instance all his sympathy went to his sister Marjorie, whom he called "Mana". She had selflessly devoted her life to trying to bring a little order into the whirlwind career of "Mac".

There had been rivalry between Micheál and his brother-in-law; if this sometimes grew into envy it was usually dispelled by loud sardonic laughter. Mary Rose McMaster recalled:

It was wonderful when my father and Micheál were together. There was a healthy rivalry between them and each would try to out-do the other with theatre stories and mimicry. Mac had a pre-occupation with stage lights and was known to re-focus them or change a gell in the middle of a scene; Micheál did a marvellous imitation of him doing this (Forever Amber!) and there was a passage in *As You Like It* that Mac could never learn so he'd have pieces of the script pinned up on the backs of trees in the forest of Arden! Micheál did an imitation of this and kept going to the wrong tree! It was hilarious! Mac also imitated Micheál who he felt posed too much on the stage and his caricature of M's Hamlet was incredible. My mother's position in all this must have been quite difficult when I think of it now. She loved Micheál and had practically brought him up, but she worshipped my father and was fiercely protective of him. Sometimes when she thought Micheál was going too far she'd quietly tell him to behave and he always did. They were both giants and when they got together they were brilliant and entertaining. I was shy and just looked and listened, in awe; my brother Christopher retreated into himself having a clear but more introspective mind of his own. In adulthood I think of it with pleasure, but it also makes the kind of talk one is usually involved in pale and uninteresting. Chris on the other hand had not happy memories of it but rather feels he was overshadowed and not allowed to express himself.[1]

It was hard for Christopher to grow in the shadow of a mighty oak, Mac, and a mighty ash, Micheál. Mary Rose, in contrast, seems happy that she saw not only Shelley plain but Byron also.

In 1963 MacLiammóir toured Australia and New Zealand and was feted in Sydney, Melbourne and Canberra. Nevertheless, he seemed unhappy. Sydney, he wrote home, was "exactly like a large packing case — it is Clapham Junction in a heatwave after one has travelled painfully around the world to get to it". In Canberra he

> opened to a diplomatic house — audience grand — but as they were all diplomats many of them pretending to know English better than they really did, do or ever will; the laughs were a little forced. On a whole, No, I don't like this country. Why not? The climate is lovely although the seasons like everything else are upside down. However, it is better than Sydney's gloomy cheerfulness but not as good as Melbourne's real (seemingly to quote Ian Priestly Mitchell) and sincere appreciation. The French wife of the Dutch ambassador was hideous but amusing; it was nice to talk French again in this monolingual desert. She looked like the Witch of Endor but talked like Lady Bracknell (in French) and was very funny.[2]

In his published account in *An Oscar of No Importance* he attributes his disillusion with Australia to the moodiness of Brian Tobin, a friend who had become manager of the Gate Company: "a personal relationship had been turned into a professional relationship" which did not work for either party.

While MacLiammóir travelled abroad, at home Hilton Edwards had joined the new television service as the first Head of Drama, and for nearly two years the Gate Company existed only in name. He soon found the administrative demands of *Telefís Éireann* restrictive and inhibiting. He was tied to a nine to five office job in Montrose, returning home each evening to slump in a chair before a television set like a tired businessman. MacLiammóir believed him to be "dying of Video Tapeworm". Eventually Edwards left his steady job in television to try to keep the Gate open. He threatened that he would put an advertisement in all the papers for "a partner in the theatre incapable of doing a one-man show"; he said, mostly in jest, that like Frankenstein he had created a monster and that this monster would destroy the Gate. In fact, some of the money which MacLiammóir earned on tour went to keeping the theatre not so much alive as ticking over. Nevertheless, as far as the Gate was concerned, Wilde had got it right as usual when he had said that nothing fails like success — in this case MacLiammóir's success.

MacLiammóir had already prepared another one-man show, developing *Stars at Midnight* into a full-length show called *I Must Be Talking to My Friends*. It was a personal anthology selected from those writers who had meant most to him. It depicted, in the words of Hilton Edwards, "the tragedy and comedy of Ireland's progress, lyrical and grotesque, wayward and pitiful, blood-stained and laughing, from an ancient to a modern civilization". It was enormously successful at Oxford and Cambridge and on the American University circuit, but it lacked the brilliant single focus of the *Oscar* show. Another solo performance, *Talking about Yeats*, prepared for the centenary of the poet's birth in 1965, was a personal tribute by the actor to his idol. Again it was welcomed in the groves of academe but it remained a wonderfully illustrated lecture rather than a piece of drama, and it later formed the basis of a book on Yeats which MacLiammóir wrote in collaboration with the poet Eavan Boland. Dame Edith Sitwell wrote to tell Micheál that "nobody else could recite the lyrics of dear Mr Yeats".

Ireland has few honours to bestow on her artists; actors of the present day do not even qualify as members of the Irish academy of arts, *Aosdána*, and the establishment is reluctant to acknowledge any player until he or she has received the acclaim of London or New York. In a country which has statues to racehorses and greyhounds in public places, there are none to actors. However, many years before his success in *The Importance of Being Oscar* two individual theatregoers, Carmel and

Shiela Leahy, with the help of their father, had presented to MacLiammóir a bronze bust of himself by the Cork sculptor Marshall Hutson RHA. The plaster-cast had been made while MacLiammóir was playing at the Cork Opera House and was later exhibited at the Royal Hibernian Academy. The sisters had always been fans of Micheál's and then they became friends, enjoying a regular correspondence with him for the rest of his life. About the Hutson bust, Micheál wrote that at the modelling stage he thought the head too saintly: "I think I look like a cross St Augustine but maybe all will change and my true demoniac nature will appear when Hutson gets to know me better". After he had been formally presented with the bust by the Leahy sisters he was more appreciative: "The head of me in bronze done by Hutson I genuinely think a triumph — it is the grandest personal tribute I have".[3] In 1957 the Leahy sisters had a plaque erected in the reconstructed Gate to commemorate the work of Edwards and MacLiammóir there; also in the theatre is a bronze head by Marjorie Fitzgibbon of MacLiammóir as an old man.

MacLiammóir was elected a member of the Irish Academy of Letters and received the Lady Gregory Medal. In 1961, when Trinity College Dublin conferred on him the honorary degree of LLD, his partner pretended to feel snubbed. Whenever the phone rang at 4 Harcourt Terrace and someone asked for "Doctor MacLiammóir", Hilton would say demurely: "He is operating abroad but this is Nurse Edwards speaking". Later the National University conferred degrees on both of them and they were jointly made Freemen of the City by Dublin Corporation. France made MacLiammóir a Chevalier of the Legion d'Honneur.

While MacLiammóir and Edwards were being honoured for their contribution to Irish theatre, the Gate remained in dire need of financial subsidy. The government presented the Abbey with a newly designed theatre in 1966, fifteen years after the fire which had destroyed the old theatre, causing Hilton Edwards to remark that "it was like putting a Christian Dior creation on a barefoot Connemara colleen". When the Abbey in its new home began to produce Goldsmith, Chekov, Shakespeare and Wilde, all of whom had up to then been regarded mainly as Gate property, Edwards threatened that he would retaliate by staging an old Abbey comedy, *The Country Dressmaker*, with MacLiammóir in the title role. For years there had been plans — some plainly quixotic — to provide for the Gate in a new theatre complex: one design envisaged three theatres on one site housing the Abbey, the Gate and the *Comhar Dramaíochta*. The Queen's Theatre, which the Abbey had occupied for fifteen years after the fire, could have been purchased and converted into a theatre suitable for the Gate, but it was demolished to make way for an office block. Eventually Charles J. Haughey, then Minister for Finance, provided a grant to the Gate Company in 1969, but the Rotunda building was found to be unsafe because of dry rot and the theatre did not reopen until March 1971. State support came late for the theatre of MacLiammóir and Edwards, but at least in its later years the Arts Council granted it an annual subvention.

In 1965 MacLiammóir had been appointed by Dr James Ryan, the Minister for Finance, as one of the twenty-five shareholders who were to act as trustees of the new Abbey and Peacock theatres. MacLiammóir was willing to do his best to help Edwards' "barefoot Connemara colleen" out of the mists of the past. Although not often free to attend, his contribution to discussions at shareholders' meetings were always helpful, humorous and well-informed. I was frequently in the chair when he spoke on such matters as the expansion of the Abbey's repertoire to include modern plays of international significance. Although such a development might provoke Edwards, MacLiammóir would set no bounds to the march of a national theatre. "Issue a manifesto," he advised. "Tell Ireland and the world that this is Liberty Hall". When someone complained that a performance had had to be cancelled because of the illness of members of the cast, Micheál interjected: "Get good understudies and none of them will get sick". Once when I explained that a government grant had been cut because the theatre had underspent its budget in the previous year, he pronounced that its was a terrible thing "not to spend every penny of a government grant". When concern was expressed at a falling-off in the quality of new plays submitted, he said that the Abbey would be foolish to expect a steady succession of masterpieces and reminded those present that "the spirit bloweth where it listeth". If what he said was not always remarkable, his short speeches were always delivered with a gracious eloquence. I noticed as he grew older that he tired easily and sometimes left before the end of a meeting, perhaps from boredom.

As he entered his mid-sixties MacLiammóir's sight deteriorated rapidly. When a New Zealand critic wrote that "Mr MacLiammóir could hold an audience spellbound by reading a telephone directory", he could not have known that MacLiammóir found it increasingly difficult to read such print. His excellent memory seldom failed him during his one-man shows; he remembered his lines, he said, by forgetting everything else. He had to forget, but not for this reason, all about stage design although he still did sketches for costumes. What has survived of his graphic work and illustration was meticulously catalogued with a perceptive commentary by Richard Pine in the catalogue for the Golden Jubilee Gate Theatre Exhibition in 1978. While he had abandoned any ambition as a serious painter MacLiammóir's work as a stage designer strongly influenced his contemporaries.

The early Beardsley influence in his art was superseded by that of Leon Bakst and Gordon Craig and with his early designs he provided not only an alternative but a challenge to naturalism. If the Fay brothers in the early years of the Abbey taught Dublin audiences how to use their ears, it was MacLiammóir who enticed them by imaginative decor to use their eyes also. This was an achievement in a city where decor had been largely neglected or ignored. Lennox Robinson, who was associated with the Abbey in various capacities for half a century, has put on record the poor visual sense of a theatre where the stage-manager usually decided on the settings and lighting and a wardrobe mistress, who seldom saw a play in its entirety, decided what the cast would wear. With considerable justice Lennox Robinson complained about "the incredibly graceless and ugly costumes" and "the green jackets, red caps trimmed with shells" which Yeats considered suitable for the demons in *The Countess Cathleen,* a play for which MacLiammóir later designed striking costumes in the 1953 Gate production. Notable exceptions to the all-pervading naturalism at the early Abbey were Charles Rickett's costumes for *On Baile's Strand* and Gordon Craig's designs — the famous screens — for *The Hour Glass* and other verse plays.

MacLiammóir took up where these innovators had left off and it was only after he had put his stamp on presentation styles at the Gate that the Abbey in the mid-thirties engaged designers like Tanya Moseivitch to improve standards. The Gate repertoire of international works allowed MacLiammóir to experiment in a wide variety of styles. Even when he tackled a design for a conventional naturalistic play, he adopted an imaginative, almost surrealistic approach which matched Hilton Edwards' skills as a director. What is often mistakenly described as a Gate style was really an eclecticism embracing a multiplicity of styles which suited a wide range of works, from Aeschylus to Anouilh and from Sophocles to Shaw. In later years, designers like Michael O'Herlihy and Carl Bonn worked in both the Gate and the Abbey theatres.

Hilton Edwards in association with Oscar Lewenstein shared a major success in the production of Brian Friel's *Philadelphia Here I Come* in Dublin and New York. First staged for the Dublin Theatre Festival in 1964, with Patrick Bedford and Donal Donnelly in the leading roles, it transferred with the same cast to New York where it had a long run followed by a coast to coast tour of the States. Another Brian Friel play, *Lovers,* produced at the Gate in 1967, transferred from the Gate to New York and Los Angeles. *The Loves of*

Cass Maguire, first staged in New York, and *Crystal and Fox*, also produced by Hilton Edwards at the Gate, were less successful. MacLiammóir had little part in the success or staging of these Friel plays although the author in a posthumous tribute credited him with the designs "for four of his plays". Friel continued: "I am not aware that I have any theatrical pedigree; but if I had to produce documentation I would be pleased to claim — to paraphrase Turgenev's comment on Gogol — that I came from under the Edwards-MacLiammóir overcoat".

While MacLiammóir was content to give up his part in stage design, the actor chaffed as the handicap imposed by poor sight made the study of new parts an unwelcome chore. He was reluctant to wear glasses and contact lenses were not recommended for his eye condition. He wore spectacles for a short time until Ulick O'Connor told him he looked like Perry Mason: this was too much for Micheál and he did not wear them again in public or in his one-man shows. While on a tour of South Africa, under the auspices of the British Council in 1967, he spent some time in hospital in Pretoria where he was nursed by Irish nuns. Despite his illness he insisted on playing *Oscar* each night. In Johannesburg he had spells of dizziness and suffered badly from the old nightmare of falling into nothingness if he stepped off the violet and gold carpet which he brought everywhere with him.

He disliked apartheid and played to blacks when and where they were permitted to attend, but he also reminded himself that "he was an actor as well as a coward". As a guest of the government he decided that he would only harm himself by playing the part of an amateur reformer, without being of the least help to "the millions of dark faces". He liked Port Elizabeth where among others he met Lady Glenavy's sister, Dorothy, the aunt of Patrick Campbell, "the only man who, among other achievements, has turned a natural stutter into a work of art". In Capetown he showed his old skill in the handling of press photographers. "When he spoke," wrote a journalist of a press conference, "he kept a shrewd publicity-conscious eye on a *Cape Times* photographer who walked round the actor angling for a good close up. Mr MacLiammóir followed the camera as deftly as a flower turns to the sun." [4]

At the Dublin Theatre Festival in 1969 MacLiammóir's appearance in an Abbey production by Sir Tyrone Guthrie of Eugene McCabe's *Swift* should have been a memorable occasion. Unfortunately, he was in bad shape physically and unable to sustain a new and unaccustomed role as Swift, the gloomy Dean of St Patrick's. Mary Rose McMaster recalls: "His sight was going and I went every day to Harcourt Terrace to help him with his lines. I would read them over and over to him because he could hardly read them for himself. I was very sad for him, he loved to read so much." [5] The script was considerably re-written during rehearsals; these changes and revisions were an additional burden for MacLiammóir. Sir Tyrone Guthrie was one of the dictator-director breed and MacLiammóir could not respond to such pressure.

"It's like trying to push a car with no juice up a hill," Guthrie told me when I asked how rehearsals were going. At the time Sir Tyrone had more or less retired to Annaghmakerrig, his old home near Newbliss, where he had become interested in local industry and had started a jam factory. Wilting under the strain, MacLiammóir groaned ruefully: "I wish he would stick to his jam!" Moreover, with his hatred of drunks, it was certainly no help that MacLiammóir had to share a stage-bed "with an actor who smelled like a brewery". The simple fact was that, in his state of health, he was miscast in the part — something that Sir Tyrone would hardly admit.

In retrospect, Hilton Edwards was clearly the only director who could cope with Micheál MacLiammóir. With Edwards now in demand elsewhere, only MacLiammóir's great spirit and courage helped him to overcome the failing of his powers. One of the best insights into the turmoil and torment he endured is given in Simon Callow's incisive and entertaining book, *Being an Actor*. As a young man Callow spent some time as a student at Queen's University, Belfast, where he studied

English. Hating academic life, he joined the Dram. Soc. in Queen's and took part in the Peoples Democracy marches of 1969. The highlight of all this drama, on and off stage, was his brief association with MacLiammóir who came to Queen's to adjudicate at the Irish University Drama Festival. As part of his fee, he was also to give two performances of *The Importance of Being Oscar*. As Simon Callow had earlier interviewed MacLiammóir for the college magazine, he was now seconded to the actor as his dresser and general factotum. According to Callow, MacLiammóir in his dressing-room was boyish, boastful and scurrilous about his gayness. But as the time of the performance approached, Callow noticed a change:

The patter became a trickle and finally dried up. His make-up — which in fact only amounted to touching-up his street make-up — was quickly affected; his costume consisted of nothing more than evening dress, and of course a green carnation. He sat in front of the mirror staring haunted at his face. He seemed barely to hear the calls. As the curtain got closer and closer, he started to tremble. Sweat trickled through his rouge. He grasped at the table in front of him till his knuckles were white. The stage-manager arrived to give him his call. He reached out for my hand. "Lead me," he said. "I can't see, d'you see." Down the pitch-dark corridor we went, his finger nails digging ruts into my palms, while with his free hand he crossed himself again and again. "Jesus, Mary and Joseph. Jesus protect me Jesus". We reached the stage. I said, "There are three stairs now". "Where? Where?" I helped him up, one, two, three. He fumbled with a black curtain drape, pushed it aside, and was on stage. In the pitch black, the light dazzled, and then Micheál's voice rock steady as if he had been on for hours; "To drift with every passion till my soul . . ." I stepped round to the front and watched the ebullient, unrecognisable figure juggle words and emotions, drawing his audience of largely middle-aged, middle-class Belfast burghers and their wives into his charmed circle, luring them into a world of sophistication and wit that they would in any other circumstances abhor, somehow making them feel that he and they shared a secret and a wisdom. He used to claim that he was a *seanchaí*, a story-teller, and here was the spell in action.[6]

The last decade of MacLiammoir's life was haunted by a dread of growing old. He had frequent reminders of mortality as he watched the slow decline of his nearest and dearest sister, Marjorie. He had paid for her treatment in an expensive nursing home and whenever he was in Dublin he visited her nearly every day. He kept his nieces, Sally Travers in London and Mary Rose McMaster in San Francisco, informed:

Now this part of the letter will be identical with one I am sending to our darling Mary Rose as it is about poor little Mana. I never believed until a couple of years ago that it would be possible to pray day and night for the death of someone I love so much. Every single day since I can remember anything at all, she, my mother, and other three sisters are my earliest and most enduring images: even our father seems a later edition (*sic*) to a very old picture gallery. As for Mana herself we have sat silently side by side through the greatest performances of Nijinsky, Pavlova, Karsavina, Bernhardt, Caruso and many others as well as sitting side by side over lesson books which through her hands and mind formed by far the greatest part of any conventional education I have received. It is horrible to see her now lying helpless in bed in almost constant pain and with every humiliation known to old age heaped upon her, and nobody who loved could but pray for her release from the body's cage that, besides, has never interested her in the least. She was always uncannily indifferent to things of the body — and I remember her since I was three and she eleven years of age. The body's raptures, ailments, and pleasures alike, seemed for years to have passed her by and that she should now be a prisoner in its trap seems doubly cruel. But I promise you that everything possible that can be done for her is being done; one of the best doctors in Dublin, Mervyn

Abramhson, attends her daily, and she has a day and night nurse and is in the best nursing home in town.[7]

Marjorie McMaster died on 7 March 1970 and Micheál, who hated funerals, wrote a moving account of the obsequies to his darling Sal:

Mana died on Saturday the 7th — of course it was the seventh of this month — at seven o'clock in the morning.

It was no surprise as she had begun to die the day before and had all the Last Rites and was finally put to rest in an elaborate and beautiful white satin quilted coffin where she looked like a very happy little doll. I was so joyful that she was suffering no longer either in mind or body and yet wept. So many friends gathered there and again on Monday at Mass which was held in the Adam and Eve church, Merchant's Quay, which looks over the Liffey to the Four Courts (I don't know if you remember, probably not, I wasn't sure myself until we got there for the removal of the coffin on Saturday) and then we all went to Dean's Grange where the tiny little coffin was put in beside Mac's. It was a lovely March day and there were so many friends and so many flowers that, remembering the suffering she had endured for so long, we all felt happy, in an odd sort of way to be sending her forth on her mysterious journey, and I know that all will be more than well with her. For she was, with a few bright, brief and bitter exceptions, a sweet good creature.

My own memories of Mana go back so far and are so all-pervading in my life that I could never forget her and all she has meant to me. When, one brief moment, she looked up and said to me in a half-dazed way, "Are you my little brother, Micheál?" I had to reassure her on that point; to remind her of Mac and Mary Rose and Chris and our father and Sophie, as well as Pavlova, Nijinsky, Karsavina, Caruso, Bernhardt and the great figures of our youth whom we had watched and listened to together.[8]

Sooner or later, everything in life, even death or burial, was related to a stage presentation by MacLiammóir. His dread of illness and old age brought back what Maud Gonne had said to him: "Micheál dear, they talk of the beauty of old age. Don't believe a word of it. It's hell!"

MacLiammóir's seventieth birthday was celebrated by a special *Late Late Show*. He told Gay Byrne that he was "exquisitely embarrassed" but, of course, he did not show the least signs of this. It was the first time that a *Late Late Show* was devoted exclusively to paying honour to a national figure. His friends and admirers in the studio audience joined over a million viewers in a unique tribute to an actor, author, painter and polyglot. He was acclaimed primarily as a creator and player of great roles: patriots and poltroons, saints and sinners, kings and paupers, the Moor and the Dane. The jewel in the crown was *The Importance of Being Oscar* and several video excerpts were shown. There were tributes from the rich and the famous, at home and abroad. There were even a few Corkmen present to claim him as one of their own. The final irony of this splendid occasion was that there could be no mention of his greatest creation — the unique Micheál MacLiammóir. Those who knew did not talk, those who talked did not know.

Apart from that night of jubilation, MacLiammóir had, understandably, reservations about television. His nephew Christopher McMaster and Hilton Edwards had directed a television production of *The Importance of Being Oscar* for Granada and Chloe Gibson did a two hour version for RTE which won a Jacob's Award. His main criticism was directed against TV drama and the spurious spontaneity of such shows as *This Is Your Life*. "I dislike television trying to bring theatre to the fireside," he once said. "It's like bringing religious sacraments to bed with the breakfast tray."

Despite the problem posed by his poor eyesight he was keen to continue acting. His last appearance with Hilton Edwards was in 1971 in Brian Phelan's *The Signalman's Apprentice* but he played in *Don Juan in Hell* at the Gate in 1973 and Hilton tried to find small parts in which he could make even a brief appearance, like that of King Charles in Desmond Forrestal's play about Saint Oliver Plunkett, *The True History of the Horrid Popish Plot*. His last appearance in a play, as distinct from a solo performance, was at Christmas 1974 when he played Lofty in Goldsmith's *The Good-Natured Man*.

On his seventy-sixth birthday President Ó Dálaigh gave a lunch in MacLiammóir's honour at Áras an Uachtaráin. Siobhán McKenna was there in a double capacity as the grande dame of the Irish theatre and, unofficially, as a member of the Council of State, and the President had also invited Michael Scott and myself to join the party. At the luncheon, MacLiammóir seemed determined to belie his years. He spoke effortlessly in Irish and English about folklore, of hawthorn blossoms and May Eve, of the boughs of the rowan tree. This was relevant to a surprise planned by the President who invited Hilton and Micheál to plant two ash trees. He hoped in time to have what he called a "Grove of the Muses" somewhere near the front entrance to the Áras, to complement the line of trees planted by notable heads of state on the other side of the building. After Micheál with some assistance had blown out twenty-five candles — roughly one for every three years — on his birthday cake, the party went to the site selected but, as it was not the time for planting ash, Hilton and Micheál drove little black crosses with their names into the ground to mark the spots where the saplings would be planted. As Micheál wielded a mallet to drive his marker into the field, Hilton implored us to keep back for fear of injuries. The trees were never planted. President Ó Dálaigh felt compelled to resign in protest against an insult by the Minister for Defence and nothing more was heard about the plans for a Grove of the Muses. However, it was not the last occasion on which President Ó Dálaigh honoured MacLiammóir.

On Saturday 13 December 1975 Micheál MacLiammóir appeared for the last time on stage at the end of a one-week run of *The Importance of Being Oscar* at the Gate Theatre. There were some in the audience who knew that at curtain fall he would finally step aside from the violet and gold carpet. I had brought my sixteen-year-old son, Brian, so that he could say in years to come that he had seen MacLiammóir on a memorable night. I had seen him, as he said himself, *"in a aisdeoir faoi dhá sholas,"* first when the sun shone on the crystal bowl in which the goldfish swam, and now I watched as the evening shadows began to close in on him. He had suffered a mild stroke a week before and had appeared against his doctor's advice. He was much feebler now than when Simon Callow had led him down the dark corridor to the stage in Belfast. His left side was partly paralyzed, the stage furniture was a mere blur, and his right hand once or twice sought the reassurance of a table or a couch. But like blind Raftery he was still

Lán dóchais is grá	Full of hope and love
Le súilibh gan solas	With eyes without light
Le ciúineas gan crá.	Patient and quiet.

As soon as he stepped on the magic carpet he looked twenty years younger. There was a touch of tragic grandeur in his triumph over his infirmities: a Lear had regained his kingdom. At the final curtain there was a standing ovation and a tribute by the President Cearbhall Ó Dálaigh.

With that last performance he left his toupee aside and, like Prospero, bade farewell to the cloud-capped towers and gorgeous palaces, and all the magic of the stage which had entranced him for nearly seventy years.

Soon after his farewell from the stage MacLiammóir underwent brain surgery for the second time. In his last years he tried to hide the ravages of time with the cosmetic aid of Leichner No. 10 but, as Hilton Edwards said, "he deceived nobody, not even himself". Edwards attributed this fear of growing old to MacLiammóir's success as a child actor — the Peter Pan who never grew up! A cruel wit had once described him, in the words of William Plomer's parody, as "a rose red pansy half as old as time". Now he did not greatly care; he had outsoared the shadow of such spite. With a charming capacity for self-deflation, he often referred to himself as an old ham.

He loved the grand flourish and the Dublin of a more spacious age; the new Dublin of concrete office blocks and even the modern architecture of his friend Michael Scott had no appeal for him. On his last appearance in London with his one-man shows at the Haymarket Theatre, he had written:

We were at a quite frightening function the other day: Irish and British Trade. Something or other in a new room, école Michael Scott — in fact it was by M.S. — like a gymnasium cum lavatory in a rather smart prison. And speeches about how to Sell things; most inspiring. Pat Scott was there. So was Brian (Tobin) and I. I can't imagine why. B said it would be good for business. But whose?[9]

The old *joie de vivre* had almost gone. Hilton and old friends like Mary Manning, Serge Phillipson, John Finegan of the *Evening Herald*, John Jordan and members of the Gate Company, Patrick Bedford, Pat McLarnon and others tried to make the black side of Micheál's existence bearable. He and Hilton continued to visit the Leahy sisters, especially at Christmas time. MacLiammóir knew now that he would never again act or paint or write or read. He fell and could scarcely walk and was confined to a downstairs room, where he sat listening to Chopin and still smoking his favourite Gauloises. MacLiammóir's last interview was given to Donncha Ó Dúlaing for his radio programme *Highways and Byeways*:

Donncha: Micheál, we are recording this interview in the dim twilight of a January evening at the turn of the year [1978].
Micheál: The dim twilight!
Donncha: You were talking about the voices saying come away! Where do you think one goes at the end of existence?
Micheál: Oh . . . you remind me of a conversation with a good friend of mine, Desmond Rushe of the *Independent*. He said to me one day quite simply "Do you believe in God, Micheál?" I said without any hesitation, "Yes, of course I do!" "Oh," he said "I wish I could say that with such simplicity and such directness". And we then went on talking about God and an after life and so on. And I said yes and that ultimately — ultimately I believed in the Christian idea

of heaven. It isn't only Christian, I know. Most religions believe in heaven. And some of the poor misguided fools believe in hell. However, I personally believe in heaven, ultimately, but I don't think we go straight there. I don't think that any of us is ready for that, and I'm sure we're not ready for hell and I don't think we ever will be. At the hands of the God of love we are supposed to go through an infinity, an eternity of ignoble torture which we, with all our sins, would not inflict, not for five minutes, let alone forever! Yet He's supposed to do that to us as a punishment for this or that, forever and ever and ever. The idea is barbarous and, to me, ludicrous. No, I believe in a system after death, but this is something very personal. I never say it to convert.

I believe in the theory of reincarnation, not necessarily on this earth but in some form in which I think that human spirit is born again into another body with all the sort of earthly experiences, the trials, the triumphs, the unhappiness, faults and everything else, what we all go through every day. It's the same system as rehearsing a play, if you like, in my profession, or as going to school in anybody's boyhood or girlhood. You go back and learn what you failed to learn before in order to pass a certain exam, and the exam, presumably, is for heaven.

MacLiammóir surely knew that Donncha Ó Dúlaing, a Corkman, would sooner or later ask a leading question.

Donncha: Micheál, you were born a Corkman.

Micheál: I was [on a rising Cork-like note].

Donncha: Where?

Micheál: Blackrock.

Donncha: Do you have any memories of your Cork childhood?

Micheál: Yes, my very early childhood. We left when I was seven. I came back from London to live in Dublin in 1917. I forget the date. My greatest friend in the world, Máire O'Keefe, on the O'Keefe side of my mother's family, died on the 7th of January, 1929 (*sic*). On the 17th of June in 1927

I met Hilton Edwards. So sevens are significant to me. A
number of fate good or bad, you know.[10]
While still maintaining the fiction of his Cork birth, he was
quick enough to escape the dangers of reminiscing about Cork
with a Corkman and to digress into a numbers game.

Shortly before he died he allowed the carefully maintained
fiction of his Irish childhood to slip for a moment when he
revealed to his grandnephew, the painter Michael Travers, that
he had in fact been born in London. It seemed that the grand
illusion was about to end but Hilton Edwards decided otherwise. Next day he called Michael Travers aside and told him to
pay no attention to what Micheál had said since he had become
very confused following his recent operation.

Micheál MacLiammóir died at seven o'clock on the
evening of 6 March 1978 in a downstairs room at 4 Harcourt
Terrace. Four days earlier he had come home from hospital to
die. It was a source of consolation to many of his friends that at
his own request he received the Last Rites of the Catholic
Church. He was laid-out on a white counterpane clasping a
crucifix in his hand.

Ireland gave him one of the most dramatic funerals since
that of Brendan Behan. On the evening of the seventh the coffin
was taken at walking pace via Leeson Street to Newman's
University Church on St Stephen's Green. Next day requiem
mass was concelebrated by the Gate theatre playwright, Fr
Desmond Forristal, Micheál's friends Fr Sean Quigley and Fr
Michael Hurley SJ, and the priests of the parish. The President
of Ireland, Doctor Patrick Hillery, and the Taoiseach, Mr Jack
Lynch, attended. Crowds gathered outside the church and on
the streets as the coffin was borne to St Fintan's cemetery
beneath the Head of Howth. Terence de Vere White, novelist,
critic and Gate Theatre director, said in a graveside tribute:
"No Irish actor, no political figure of our time, was so loved".
Cearbhall Ó Dálaigh, on crutches after an accident, related in
Irish how MacLiammóir had chosen his last resting place
beneath the cromlech of Diarmuid and Gráinne on Beann

Eadair. Sally Travers and her nephew Michael Travers on behalf of the family thanked Hilton for all his help and Micheál for all the laughter. His only surviving sister, Peg, then in a nursing home in the South of England, could not attend. Patrick Bedford threw a green carnation on the coffin, saying, "Good night, sweet prince and flights of angels sing thee to thy rest". Hilton Edwards bade farewell with the lines from "Cymbeline":

Fear no more, the heat o' the sun
Nor the furious winter rages
Thou thy worldly task has done
Home are gone and ta'en thy wages.
Golden lads and girls all must
As chimney sweepers come to dust.

Now that he was gone, the media raised a monument of verbal tributes to the memory of MacLiammóir. There are artists of international status whose work transcends political and national boundaries, so much so that their place of origin scarcely matters. Other artists wrap their identity so closely in an adopted culture that it is indeed a shock when one learns where they were actually born. MacLiammóir's double nature bridged both categories. His claim to have given "All for Hecuba" was not braggadacio but the motto of a man who with the zeal of the convert showed Ireland what a living theatre could be.

The gradual transformation from little Alfred Willmore reading his first stage direction, "Enter a goldfish", to the final creation of the legend named MacLiammóir constituted a performance of an originality that sets it apart from the work of any other actor of his generation. Such acting transcends the story the *seanchaí* told.

In his books MacLiammóir gave an actor's version of himself, no more "real" perhaps than the theatrical roles he played. The words on the page are but part of the imaginative process which shaped his greatest creation — himself. Even the word "memoir" has an ironic ring about it as time and again the writer gave place to the *seanchaí* to embroider what he chose to remember and to keep silent about what he wanted to forget. MacLiammóir wore his frailty on his sleeve; for him art was partly myth, an invention about truth and a bridge to a golden age. He walked a fine line between the imagined and the real; it was part of the neo-romanticism which he created in the theatre. For a time such imaginative exuberance was held in low esteem by critics, but mere fashions inevitably change.

A man of marble holds the throne
With looks composed and resolute
Till death, a prince whom princes own,
Draws near to touch the marble mute.

The play is over: good my friends!
Murmur the pale lips: *Your applause*!
With what a grace the actor ends:
How loyal to dramatic laws!

A brooding beauty on his brow
Irony brooding over sin:
The next imperial actor now
Bids the satiric piece begin.[11]

CURTAIN UP

MacLiammóir, *The Importance of Being Oscar*, last appearance on stage,
December 1975   (Fergus Bourke)

Books by Micheál MacLiammóir

Autobiographical

All for Hecuba: An Irish Theatrical Autobiography, Methuen 1946.
Put Money in Thy Purse: The Filming of Orson Welles Othello, Routledge and Keegan Paul 1952.
Each Actor on His Ass, Routledge and Keegan Paul 1961.
An Oscar of No Importance, Heinemann 1968.
Enter a Goldfish: Memoirs of an Irish Actor Young and Old, Thames and Hudson 1977.

Irish

Oidhcheanta Sidhe (Faery Nights), Talbot Press 1922.
Lá agus Óidhche (Day and Night) Oifig and tSoláthair 1929.
Ceo Meala Lá Seaca (A Honeyed Mist on a Frosty Day), Sáirséal agus Dill 1952.
Aisdeoirí idir Dhá Sholas (Actors Between Spotlights), Sáirséal agus Dill 1956.
Bláth agus Taibhse (Flower and Ghost), Sáirséal agus Dill 1964.

Plays

Ill Met By Moonlight, Duffy 1964.
Where Stars Walk, Progress House 1962.
The Importance of Being Oscar, Dolmen 1963.
Óidhche Bealtaine (May Eve), Oifig an tSoláthair 1932.
Lulu, Oifig an tSoláthair 1933.
Diarmuid agus Gráinne, Oifig an tSoláthair 1935.

Other

Theatre in Ireland, Dept. of External Affairs 1950.
Ireland (with E. Smith), Thames and Hudson 1966.
W.B. Yeats and His World (with Eavan Boland), Thames and Hudson 1977.

Bibliography

Simon Callow, *Being an Actor*, Methuen 1984.

John Coulter, *In My Day*, Toronto 1980.

John Cowell, *No Profit But the Name: The Longfords and the Gate Theatre*, O'Brien 1988.

Hilton Edwards, *The Mantle of Harlequin*, Progress House 1958.

W.J. Feeney, *A Drama in Hardwicke Street*, Fairleigh Dickinson University Press 1980.

Denis Gwynn, *Edward Martyn and the Irish Revival*, Jonathan Cape 1939.

Hugh Hunt, *The Abbey Theatre*, Gill and Macmillan 1979.

Charles Higham, *Orson Welles*, St Martin's Press 1985.

Bulmer Hobson (ed.), *The Gate Theatre*, Gate Theatre 1934.

Robert Hogan, *After the Irish Renaissance*, University of Minnesota Press 1967.

Robert Hogan and Michael J. O'Neill (eds.), *Joseph Holloway's Irish Theatre*, 3 Vols, Proscenium Press 1968/'69.

Barbara Leaming, *Orson Welles: A Biography*, Penguin 1987.

Denis Johnson, *Selected Plays*, Colin Smythe 1983.

Christine Longford, *Printed Cotton: A Novel*, Methuen 1935.

Peter Luke (ed.), *Enter Certain Players: Edwards, MacLiammóir and the Gate 1928-1978*, Dolmen Press 1978.

Ria Mooney, *Players and Painted Stage: The Autobiography of Ria Mooney Part One*, Proscenium Press 1978.

Sean O'Casey, *Innisfallen Fare Thee Well*, Macmillan 1949.

Sean O'Casey, *Sunset and Evening Star*, Macmillan 1954.

Donncha Ó Dúlaing, *Voices of Ireland*, RTE 1984.

Richard Pine (ed.), *All for Hecuba, Gate Theatre Jubilee Catalogue 1978*.

Lennox Robinson (ed.), *The Irish Theatre*, Macmillan 1939.

Lennox Robinson (ed.), *Lady Gregory's Journals*, Putnam's 1946.

Lennox Robinson, *Ireland's Abbey Theatre: A History 1899-1951*, Sidgwick and Jackson 1951.

W.B Yeats, *Plays and Controversies*, Macmillan 1923.

W.B Yeats, *Essays and Introductions*, Macmillan 1961.

Notes

Prologue: A Famous First Night
1. *The Importance of Being Oscar*, preface to stage text p.ix.

Exit a Goldfish
1. *Supplement to Irish Families*
2. *All for Hecuba* p.39
3. Mary Rose McMaster, letter to the author 6 Dec. 1988.
4. *Enter a Goldfish* p.9
5. *ibid.* p.13
6. *Enter Certain Players* p.82
7. *ibid.* p.82
8. *Enter a Goldfish* p.49
9. *ibid.* p55
10. *Ceo Meala Lá Seaca* p.18
11. *Enter a Goldfish* p.55
12. The *Star* 29 Jun. 1915
13. The *Standard* 26 Jun. 1912
14. The *Sketch* 26 Jun. 1912
15. *Enter a Goldfish* pp.76-77
16. *Oscar Welles: A Biography* p.42
17. *Enter a Goldfish* p.83
18. *ibid.* p.84
19. *ibid.* p.77
20. *ibid.* p.105
21. The *Star* 29 Jun. 1915
22. *ibid.*
23. *ibid.*
24. *Enter a Goldfish* p.113
25. *ibid.* pp.115-116
26. *ibid.* p.117

The Wearing of the Green
1. *Ceo Meala Lá Seaca* p.28
2. *Essays and Introductions* pp. 203-205
3. *Enter a Goldfish* p.124

4. *ibid.* p.124
5. *ibid.* p.125
6. *Ceo Meala Lá Seaca* p.30
7. *Enter a Goldfish* p.129
8. *Essays and Introductions* p. 205
9. *Ceo Meala Lá Seaca* p.27
10. *Enter a Goldfish* p.140
11. *Evening Telegraph* 29 April 1919
12. *Joseph Holloway's Diaries*, National Library of Ireland Ms. 1845 pp. 638-639
13. *Theatre in Ireland* pp.19-20
14. *Enter a Goldfish* p.144
15. *Enter a Goldfish* p.145
16. *Essays and Introductions* p.206

The Magic Mountain
1. Cambridge Theatre Festival programme 26 Oct. 1931.
2. *La agus Óidhche* pp.107-108
3. *Enter a Goldfish* p.183
4. *All for Hecuba* p.13
5. *ibid.* p.15
6. *ibid.* p.19

Not Only Gaelic, But Free!
1. *Each Actor on His Ass* p.245
2. *All for Hecuba* p.27
3. *Enter a Goldfish* p.189
4. *Joseph Holloway's Irish Theatre, Vol.1* pp. 29-30
5. *Poems and Prose* p.77
6. *Joseph Holloway's Irish Theatre, Vol.1* p.31
7. *All for Hecuba* p.52
8. *ibid.* p.53
9. *ibid.* p.53
10. *ibid.* p.54
11. *ibid.* p.54
12. *ibid.* pp.54-55
13. *Connacht Sentinel* 28 Aug. 1928

The Starting Gate
1. *Gate Jubilee catalogue* p.44
2. *Lady Gregory's Journals* pp.115-116
3. *Gate Jubilee catalogue* p.4
4. *Sunset and Evening Star* p.105
5. *All for Hecuba* p.73
6. *ibid.* pp.73-74
7. *ibid.* p.74
8. *ibid.* p.95

Theatre Business
1. *All for Hecuba* pp.172-173
2. *ibid.* p.173
3. *No Profit But the Name*
4. *All for Hecuba* pp.34-35
5. *ibid.* p.134
6. *Orson Welles: A Biography* p.43
7. *All for Hecuba* p.163
8. *ibid.* p.163
9. *Joseph Holloway's Irish Theatre, Vol. 1* p.6
10. The *Irish Monthly*, Mar. 1932
11. The *Irish Statesman*, 6 Feb. 1932
12. The *Irish Independent*, 3 Feb. 1932
13. *All for Hecuba* p.221
14. *ibid.* p.221
15. *Motley* Feb. 1933
16. *Printed Cotton*, p.101

Masks and Faces
1. Mary Rose McMaster, letter to the author 18 Dec. 1988.
2. *Orson Welles: A Biography* p.72
3. *Enter a Goldfish* p.191
4. *ibid.* pp.190-191
5. Micheál MacLiammóir, undated letter to Carmel and Shiela Leahy.
6. *All for Hecuba* p.172
7. *Enter Certain Players* p.10

8. *All for Hecuba* p.349
9. *Motley* April/May 1933
10. *The Irish Theatre* pp.126-218
11. Mary Rose McMaster, undated letter to the author.
12. *ibid.*
13. *Irish Press* 26 Nov. 1940

Hadn't We the Gaiety
1. *Theatre in Ireland* p.55
2. *Gate Jubilee catalogue* p.5
3. *Sunset and Evening Star* p.97
4. *Put Money in Thy Purse* p.78
5. *Enter Certain Players* p.78
6. Micheál MacLiammóir, letter to Sally Travers 9 Jan. 1973.
7. *Dublin Magazine* Oct./Dec. 1947
8. *All for Hecuba* p.154
9. *The Theatre Advancing* p. 23

No Money in Thy Purse!
1. *Put Money in Thy Purse* v
2. *ibid.* vii
3. *ibid.* p.92
4. *ibid.* p.77
5. *Each Actor on His Ass* pp.11-12
6. Micheál MacLiammóir, letter to Carmel and Shiela Leahy 1958.
7. From W.B. Yeats "The Old Stone Cross", *Last Poems*.
8. *All for Hecuba* p.11

The Reingreencarnation
1. *An Oscar of No Importance* p.3
2. *ibid.* p.3
3. *ibid.* pp.57-58
4. *The Importance of Being Oscar*, stage text pp.9, 15, 39

Our Revels Now Are Ended
1. Mary Rose McMaster, letter to the author 1988.
2. Micheál MacLiammóir, letter to Carmel and Shiela Leahy 2 June 1963.

3. Micheál MacLiammóir, undated letter to Carmel and Shiela Leahy.
4. The *Cape Times*
5. Mary Rose McMaster, undated letter to the author.
6. *Being an Actor* pp.21-22
7. Micheál MacLiammóir, undated letter to Sally Travers.
8. *ibid.*
9. Micheál MacLiammóir, undated letter to Carmel and Shiela Leahy.
10. *Voices of Ireland* pp.47-49
11. "The Roman Stage", *The Complete Poems of Lionel Johnson.*

REGISTRATION DISTRICT _Cork_

BIRTH in the Sub-district of _Dillons_ in the _Cork of Middlesex_

No.	When and where born	Name, if any	Sex	Name and surname of father	Name, surname and maiden surname of mother	Occupation of father	Signature, description and residence of informant	When registered	Signature of registrar	Name entered after registration
	Columns:—	1	2	3	4	5	6	7	8	9	10
4	Second Fifth October 1899 at 150 Purves Road N.W.6	Alfred Lee Willmore	Boy	Alfred Lloyd Willmore Lee	Mary Elizabeth Lee formerly Dillon	Willman Tailor & Shop keeper	W.L. Willmore Lee father Mother December 1899 150 Purves Road	Twenty Fifth 1899 Register Lee	Willmore Registrar	

CERTIFIED to be a true copy of an entry in the certified copy of a Register of Births in the District above mentioned.
Given at the GENERAL REGISTER OFFICE, LONDON, under the Seal of the said Office, the _19th_ day of _February_ 1988

Birth certificate of Alfred Lee Willmore—Micheál MacLiammóir

CERTIFIED COPY OF AN ENTRY OF BIRTH

GIVEN AT THE GENERAL REGISTER OFFICE, LONDON

Application Number PAS 3.2.0.265/12/57

REGISTRATION DISTRICT Marylebone

BIRTH in the Sub-district of Hampstead in the County of Middlesex

No.	When and where born	Name, if any	Sex	Name and surname of father	Name, surname and maiden surname of mother	Occupation of father	Signature, description and residence of informant	When registered	Signature of registrar	Name entered after registration
193	Twenty-third May 1953 57 Eton Avenue	Alfred George	Boy		Eliza Willmore		E. Willmore, Mother, 57 Eton Avenue, N.W.3	Fourth June 1953	J. Sugden Registrar	

CERTIFIED to be a true copy of an entry in the certified copy of a Register of Births in the District above mentioned.
Given at the GENERAL REGISTER OFFICE, LONDON, under the Seal of the said Office, the 5th day of December 1957

BXB 688255

This certificate is issued in pursuance of the Births and Deaths Registration Act 1953. Section 34 provides that any certified copy of an entry purporting to be sealed or stamped with the seal of the General Register Office shall be received as evidence of the birth or death to which it relates without any further or other proof of the entry, and no certified copy purporting to have been given in the said Office shall be of any force or effect unless it is sealed or stamped as aforesaid.

CAUTION—It is an offence to falsify a certificate or to make or knowingly use a false certificate or a copy of a false certificate intending it to be accepted as genuine to the prejudice of any person or to possess a certificate knowing it to be false without lawful authority.

Birth certificate of Alfred George Willmore

CERTIFIED COPY OF AN ENTRY OF BIRTH

GIVEN AT THE GENERAL REGISTER OFFICE, LONDON

Application Number. PAS 320269/1/89

REGISTRATION DISTRICT *Islington*

1867 BIRTH in the Sub-district of *Islington East* in the *County of Middlesex*

Columns:—	1	2	3	4	5	6	7	8	9	10*
No.	When and where born	Name, if any	Sex	Name and surname of father	Name, surname and maiden surname of mother	Occupation of father	Signature, description and residence of informant	When registered	Signature of registrar	Name entered after registration
200	*Twenty-ninth July 1867 4 Stanley Lane Med J*	*Mary Elizabeth*	*Girl*	*Robert Samuel Lee*	*Rebecca Lee formerly Ross*	*Working Jeweller*	*R. S. Lee Father 8 Arlington Street Arlington*	*Thirty-first August 1867*	*Worthington Registrar*	

*See note overleaf

CERTIFIED to be a true copy of an entry in the certified copy of a Register of Births in the District above mentioned.
Given at the GENERAL REGISTER OFFICE, LONDON, under the Seal of the said Office, the *8th* day of *December* 1989

BXB 688271

This certificate is issued in pursuance of the Births and Deaths Registration Act 1953. Section 34 provides that any certified copy of an entry purporting to be sealed or stamped with the seal of the General Register Office shall be received as evidence of the birth or death to which it relates without any further or other proof of the entry, and no certified copy purporting to have been given in the said Office shall be of any force or effect unless it is sealed or stamped as aforesaid.

CAUTION:—It is an offence to falsify a certificate or to make or knowingly use a false certificate or a copy of a false certificate intending it to be accepted as genuine to the prejudice of any person or to possess a certificate knowing it to be false without lawful authority.

Form A5041 Dd 8898392 864095 90M 4/89 Mid(337407)

Birth certificate of Mary Elizabeth Lee

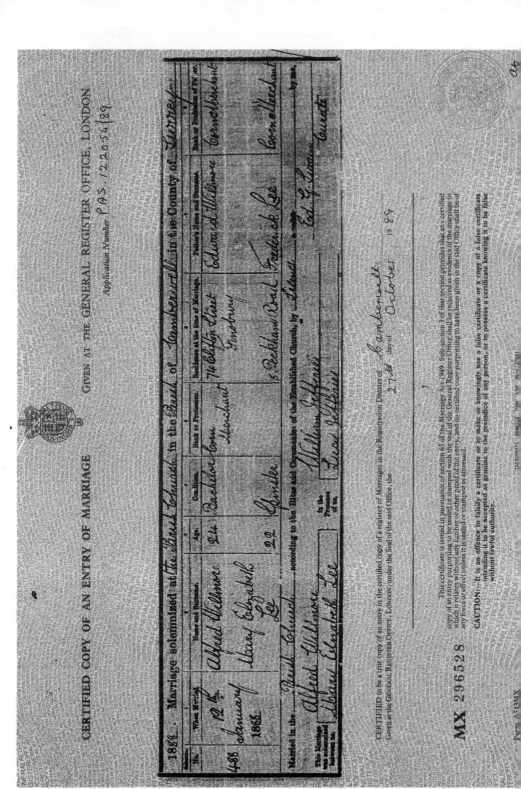

Marriage certificate of Alfred George Willmore and Mary Elizabeth Lee